Men and Abortion:
A Path to Healing

Men and Abortion

A Path to Healing

C.T. COYLE, Ph.D.

LIFE CYCLE BOOKS
Toronto, ON • Lewiston, NY

Men and Abortion: A Path to Healing

ISBN: 0-919225-23-3

Published by:
Life Cycle Books
P.O. Box 420
Lewiston, NY 14092-0420

Phone: (800) 214-5849
Fax: (888) 690-8532
e-mail: orders@lifecyclebooks.com
web site: www.lifecyclebooks.com

Canadian Office:
Life Cycle Books Ltd.
421 Nugget Ave. Unit 8
Toronto, ON M1S 4L8

Printed in Canada

Contents

Acknowledgments 7
Preface. 8

PART ONE: BACKGROUND

Dan's Story 13
1. Legalized Abortion: Impact on Men 19
2. Post-Abortion Stress in Men. 29
3. Forgiveness: A Psychological Model 37

Matthew's Story. 53
4. Forgiveness: A Christian Imperative 57

Chris' Story 65

PART TWO: HEALING AFTER ABORTION

Jack's Story 71
5. Anger and Forgiveness 75

Ted's Story. 87
6. Helplessness and Forgiveness 91

Bill's Story. 99
7. Guilt and Forgiveness 103

Cal's Story *117*
8. Relationship Problems and Forgiveness. 121
Paul's Story *131*
9. Grief and Forgiveness. 133
David's Story *145*
10. Helping Others to Heal 147

Appendix A 155
Testing a Healing Program for Post-Abortion Men

Appendix B 163
Processes of Forgiving Another

Appendix C 165
Post-Abortion Resources

Endnotes *169*

Acknowledgments

THERE ARE SEVERAL PEOPLE who have contributed directly to this work and to whom I am most grateful. Dr. Robert Enright, president of the International Forgiveness Institute, was both advisor and collaborator in the research on which this book is based. His commitment to the noble task of forgiveness remains a source of inspiration.

Vicki Thorn, Dr. Vincent Rue, and Dr. David Reardon each offered helpful ideas and suggestions regarding the actual manuscript. Each of these individuals is recognized as an expert in the area of post-abortion trauma and healing. All of them have devoted considerable amounts of their time and resources to the study and/or practice of post-abortion healing. Their input has been invaluable.

Above all, I want to thank the men who have so generously shared their personal stories. With deep appreciation, respect, and gratitude, this book is dedicated to those men. May their willingness to share be a blessing to many.

Preface

IN SPITE OF THE FACT that over 37 million abortions have been performed in the United States since 1973, little attention has been given to the effects of abortion on men. Nonetheless, it is apparent to many of us that there are countless men who have been deeply wounded by an abortion experience. They often suffer in silence because they are confused about their feelings, trying to put up a strong front, and ignored by a society which does not recognize the validity of their pain. These men deserve to be recognized and to have their pain acknowledged. They need to be reassured that their reactions are normal and that there is hope for their healing.

To that end, an intervention program was developed specifically for men who identified themselves as having been hurt by abortion. The program was then tested and found to be effective. This book is based on that research and may be used by post-abortion men, their families, and/or those who counsel them.

Part One provides background information. This includes information pertaining to both legal issues and the potential effects of abortion on men. There is also a description of a process model of forgiveness as it may be applied to the post-abortion man. Part One concludes with a chapter concerning forgiveness in the context of the Christian faith.

Part Two discusses the actual components of the program on which this book is based. Anger, helplessness, guilt, relationship problems, and grief are recognized as normal reactions to abortion, and forgiveness is offered as a means to find healing. The final chapter focuses on how post-abortion men can effectively reach out to others who have been similarly injured.

The majority of this book has been written in the third person while the chapter summaries in Part Two have been written in the second person. This was deliberate as the summaries entitled, "Putting the Ideas into Practice," are aimed specifically at men who have been hurt by abortion. These summaries consist of practical suggestions that post-abortion men can utilize to progress along *a path to healing.*

Part One:

BACKGROUND

Dan's Story

"WHEN I LOOK INTO my newborn daughter's eyes, the memories of what happened 12 years ago hurt even worse. She is so beautiful, so complete, as I'm sure her brother or sister would have been. God has truly touched and blessed both my wife and me. Someday, as much as I don't want to, I've decided to tell my daughter of how her mother and I did the unthinkable; we had an abortion. I'll do it because I want her to know that even good people can get caught up in bad circumstances at times. And if she, one of her friends, or even her children ever encounter 'bad circumstances,' through my unfortunate experience and daily torture, she might hopefully be advised it would be best to follow the heart and not the head by not having an abortion.

"My future wife and I had a perfect first year. Although we lived in separate cities, we saw each other at least every other week-end. When one of us would leave, we would leave notes that would be found days later. We called and wrote almost every day. It was a fun, sexy, romantic, and exciting relationship. I had never been so happy in my life – we were in love. After going steady for 11 months, I proposed marriage to her. I chose the eve of Valentine's Day because, besides being the romantic thing to do, it was also my birthday. At midnight, I asked her to marry me. She was shocked and I didn't really get a definite 'yes,' but it didn't matter because I loved her so much. I knew we would be together, forever!

"I didn't know it at the time, but she was already having morning sickness. After much thought, she found the courage to tell me something was wrong. She wanted to buy a home pregnancy test to find out for sure if her presumption was correct. I saw no harm in that, and actually, I rather relished the thought of being married and having a baby. I've always loved children and knew someday I would like to have a family. After all, I had already proposed, we were both finished with college and gainfully employed, she was actively looking for a job in the city I lived in, and we knew we loved each other. What could possibly be the problem even if she was pregnant? Or so I thought. The result of the home test affirmed her greatest fear – it was positive.

"Her response was swift, to the point, and unwavering. 'I have to get an abortion,' she said. I couldn't believe my ears. In fact, knowing her as I do, I still find it hard to believe she would even think of such a thing. She was a devout Christian. She was an honor student in high school. She was very popular and outgoing. She had attended one of the most prestigious universities in the country. She wouldn't hurt a fly. All of her friends and relatives held her in very high regard – could she actually be serious? We were in love; totally happy; I thought she must be kidding.

"In retrospect, I guess that was the problem. How could she have made such a mistake they would ask, or think? What would it do to her reputation? She couldn't handle the thought of losing the respect and admiration she had come to know from everyone that knew her.

"I tried to talk her out of it for nearly two weeks. We spent hours upon hours on the phone, but deep down I knew she wouldn't change her mind because she couldn't. Growing up as the 'perfect' eldest child of a very Catholic family and being the person all of her younger brothers and sisters looked up to, the humiliation she felt she would have to endure from her close friends, not to mention not being able to face her parents, wouldn't allow her to make the decision [not to abort]. I now know, she would rather have made the right decision – life for the fetus.

"The pressure to be a 'man of the eighties' was intense. I knew all she wanted was a shoulder to cry on, but I couldn't bring myself to giving it to her yet. She was breaking my heart. How could someone who loves you so much do that? I just wasn't ready to console her.

"It was April. She told her friends that she was going out of town to visit me for the weekend. She had done that often, so nothing looked suspicious. She drove to where I lived and stayed overnight. We talked and cried, and cried and talked for most of the night. On Saturday we drove to the clinic. She wanted me to come in but I couldn't. I sat in the parking lot and waited. It was the longest wait of my life. My head was whirling. I thought of all the good times we had had together. I wondered if our relationship could endure this, and then I curled up in the seat of my car as best I could and prayed.

"She came out of nowhere. It startled me a bit. I guess I was half asleep, but at least it was over, we could go home and get on with our lives now. I felt a sense of relief for her. I asked her if she was okay. She just looked at me. I could tell something was wrong. It was. She told me she would have to come back because the doctor thought the fetus was more than 12 weeks old. They couldn't do it today, a different, more time-consuming technique was necessary. So, the nightmare would continue for another week. I wasn't happy about it, but what could I do? We drove back to my house, and then she drove home.

"Again, I couldn't believe it. Wasn't this just our luck? Would my whole life be in turmoil now? Was this God's punishment, or His way of saying, 'Wait, this is a mistake, don't do this.' I chose the latter. I thought this was my opportunity to talk her out of it; now I could say it was a sign from God.

"No such luck. The following Friday we found ourselves back at the clinic. She had something put inside of her and was told to go and rest, so we checked into a local motel.

"She was showing a little by now. We were lying on one of the beds in the motel room. The silence was frightening. I could tell she was very scared. I wondered if she, or I for that matter, could get some sort of counseling. I rubbed her stomach and pictured the baby gasping for air inside of her. I was dying myself, but by now I knew I had to be strong for her. She seemed to be in a trance, mostly just staring. She looked sad and very numb. She was past the point of trying to justify the abortion. We didn't talk. I felt bad for her, and for us.

"My paternal instincts began kicking in, but I didn't show it. In my heart, I wanted to somehow stop the procedure and save the baby. I felt so helpless. I rubbed and rubbed her stomach thinking I could soothe the baby, or at least let it know it was loved, if just for a short time. I wanted to hold it. I wanted to hug it. I wanted it to live, like the baby chicks and rabbits I had nursed back to life as a child. I wanted to die in its place. Sadness overcame every muscle in my body... it was just so sad!

"Don't let anyone tell you, 'you will forget!' You won't forget. Each year I figure out how old my child would be if we hadn't had the abortion. I have to figure it out because for most of the year I try to suppress the fact that it ever happened. It doesn't work, but it's easier to deal with that way. Sometimes I picture its little limbs being ripped apart by the doctor and I tell myself, 'you had no choice,' but it doesn't make any difference. I don't blame my wife. It was her body and her choice to make under the circumstances as she perceived them. What's done is done... I still love her dearly. And by the way, the child would have been 12 years old on or near October 5th.

"Someday, I may go back to the city where the abortion took place and erect a gravestone in memory of the child who never got to breathe, and laugh, and play with the father and mother that would have loved him so very much. For now, I'll play with my children and think of what might have been. At least I can get some sympathy when I need it. But as much as I'd like to help, for the most part, my wife cries alone.

"So, what's the answer to the abortion question? Who knows; it just may be the epitome of rhetorical questions. As long as our society says abortion is a viable form of birth control, nothing will change. And what if it doesn't change? How many men will have to go through their lives like me, frustrated with the fact that they had or have absolutely no say in one of the most important matters of their lives – of putting their own flesh and blood to death. Why don't men have legal options? And how might it work if they did?

"I never thought I'd say this, and I'm really not sure I want to because there will always be extenuating circumstances, but the answer might simply be to, once again, stop the options. We might need to take a couple steps backward, provide more pre-marital sex education, and live with our mistakes – literally! Diseases, such as AIDS, will be forcing the issue soon regardless of Roe v. Wade, or any other legislation."

Chapter One

LEGALIZED ABORTION: IMPACT ON MEN

HOW IS IT THAT DAN and so many other men have found themselves in such a painful situation? Prior to 1973, state laws recognized the personhood of the unborn and most states limited abortion to extreme cases, particularly when the mother's physical life was threatened by the pregnancy. However, two decisions made by the United States Supreme Court on January 22, 1973, overturned the laws of individual states.[1,2] The court decided that a woman had a legal right to terminate her pregnancy within the context of a newly articulated constitutional "right to privacy" and also that an unborn child is not a "person" as the term is used in the Fourteenth Amendment. Furthermore, the court defined a threat to a mother's health so broadly as to include emotional, psychological, and familial factors.

These U.S. Supreme Court decisions also effectively denied natural fathers any rights in the abortion controversy. The decision to abort was placed in the hands of the woman and her physician and ultimately, the woman could decide to obtain an abortion for any reason at any time during her pregnancy. During the next two years, 12 states adopted spousal consent laws requiring the husband's agreement before a wife could obtain an abortion. These laws were evaluated by the Supreme Court in 1976 and the court determined that these laws were inconsistent with Roe v. Wade and therefore unconstitutional.[3] In other words, the Supreme Court decided that a husband had no legal right to limit his wife's decision to abort, or even to be informed of her decision.

There were legal scholars who disagreed with the high court's decision. Wardle and Wood noted that in the past, when conflicts between the rights of two parties occurred (such as in divorce or custody disputes), the courts tried to balance the interests of each party.[4] Witherspoon claimed that by giving the mother complete power in the abortion decision, the father's civil rights were being denied.[5] A sociologist, Amitai Etzoni, pointed out that families have become more and more vulnerable to disintegration. He further argued that denying the wishes of the father in an abortion decision would only add more stress to the fragile family structure.[6] Dr. Bernard Nathanson, a physician who formerly performed abortions, stated that "it seems manifestly unfair to say that women have exclusive rights when the consequences of abortion involve both sexes."[7]

Others have argued that if a man does not have any right in determining the occurrence of abortion, then he should not be held financially responsible when the woman chooses to carry the child to term against the man's wishes. One of the people who agreed with this argument was Karen DeCrow, a former president of the National Organization for Women. In a letter to the editor of *New York*

Times Magazine, DeCrow stated that "if a woman makes a unilateral decision to bring pregnancy to term, and the biological father does not, and cannot share in this decision, he should not be liable for 21 years of support. Or, put another way, autonomous women making independent decisions about their lives should not expect men to finance their choice."[8] Ms. DeCrow's statement is especially interesting given the fact that the National Organization for Women has long claimed that women have a 'right' to obtain legal abortions.

It is noteworthy that in cases of adoption, most states require that the natural father, whether or not he is married to the mother, be notified of the impending adoption. If the father has maintained contact with the child, some states also require his written consent before the adoption can take place. Some attorneys have argued that there should be no difference between unmarried fathers' rights concerning adoption and their rights concerning abortion.

In sum then, whether they are married to the mothers of their unborn children or not, men have no legal rights or power in an abortion decision. It is ironic that the same generation of women which has called for men to be more nurturing has also denied men the ability to protect their children.

There is very little published research regarding the consequences of abortion for men. What research exists, however, strongly suggests that some men experience traumatic and stress-related reactions after abortion. It also appears that the male's reaction to abortion is somewhat similar to that of the female in that he may experience guilt, regret, sadness, and a sense of loss. When the abortion occurs against the man's wishes, he also may experience profound feelings of helplessness and anger. There is also evidence that men tend to repress their emotional reactions to the abortion much more so than do women.[9]

Only a few years after the legalization of abortion, an article was published by Gordon and Kilpatrick in which they describe a program of group counseling for males who accompanied females to an abortion clinic.[10] The authors identified the following emotions as being commonly experienced by most of the men: anxiety, helplessness, guilt, regret, and confusion regarding responsibility. The men were also observed to be using the following defense mechanisms: denial, projection, intellectualization, and withdrawal.

Defense mechanisms are, very simply, ways we attempt to deal with unpleasant experiences or conflicts. When we are faced with a conflict, such as a reprimand from a boss, it is normal to feel uncomfortable emotions such as anger or anxiety. To deal with both the conflict and the accompanying emotions, we may use one or more defense mechanisms.

"Denial" is one such defense mechanism. When we deny what we are actually feeling, we avoid a painful emotion. A person in denial is actually unaware of some aspect of reality that he doesn't want to face. "Projection," another defense mechanism, occurs when we attribute to others what we are feeling ourselves. For example, a freshman college student who is feeling anxious about leaving home and living in a dormitory may notice fear among the other new students but not within herself. "Intellectualization" is still another defense mechanism in which the individual may spend a good deal of time thinking about the conflict but without actually experiencing the unpleasant emotions attached to the conflict. Finally, "withdrawal" is just as it sounds. The individual deliberately withdraws from thinking or speaking about the conflict and his feelings.

There are many defense mechanisms and all of them serve the same purpose which is to protect ourselves from a perceived threat. An unacceptable emotion, such as fear or guilt, may itself be perceived as a threat to our self-esteem.

We all use defense mechanisms to varying degrees and they are not necessarily unhealthy. In fact, some defense mechanisms, such as humor or suppression, are healthy and adaptive. Gordon & Kilpatrick are simply identifying the defense mechanisms they observed among a group of men waiting for their partners in an abortion clinic. These same defense mechanisms may or may not be observed among post-abortion men in general. These authors made another interesting observation. They stated that "many clients said they did not express their feelings to their partners and instead felt the need to be a source of support by presenting a strong front."[11]

This desire, on the part of men, to support their partners rather than discuss their own emotions, was also observed by Shostak & McLouth.[12] These authors point out that "the typical man rushes to placate his partner, repress his emotions, and take his cues from an environment that others structure for him."[13] In another study in which men were interviewed in an abortion clinic, it was found that 77% of the men believed that the most valuable way they could help their partners was by maintaining control over their own emotions.[14]

This tendency of men to hide their feelings may cost them dearly months or even years later. Some investigators have looked at the consequences of adolescent pregnancy and its resolution as evidenced in adulthood.[15] These researchers were attempting to discover how an unplanned pregnancy which occurred during a man's teen-age years might affect his adult life. They predicted that the greatest psychological distress would be observed among those adult men who became fathers and married their girlfriends during adolescence and that those adult men who became fathers in adolescence but did not marry would show the next highest levels of distress scores. They also expected that those men whose teen-age girlfriends had abortions would demonstrate even less psychological distress and that those men who had never experienced an unplanned teen-age pregnancy would evidence the least amount of distress. As hypothesized, the psychological distress scores were lowest among adult males who had never experienced an adolescent pregnancy. However, an unexpected finding was that the men whose partners had abortions were more distressed than the men who became fathers. This finding remained constant whether the men who experienced abortion were compared to either the men who married their pregnant partners or to the men who remained single fathers. In other words, abortion during adolescence, rather than unplanned parenthood (with or without marriage), was the most stressful experience and this stress was evident years later during adulthood.

Those who counsel men have also observed post-abortion stress among them. One counselor acknowledged that there exists an "inherent feeling of unfairness" in the abortion decision in spite of the fact that it is a woman's legal right.[16] This may contribute to the post-abortion man's anger and also support his belief that he must contain his own emotions in order to avoid further upsetting the woman. Another counselor remarked that the emotions men have are many and varied. "Some are angry and upset with themselves and/or their partner for being in this situation. Others may be afraid or feel guilty; believing abortion is murder, they fear being an accomplice. I mentioned earlier how some men may feel helpless and powerless, not knowing what to do and having little input. A general sense of sadness and regret is prevalent among men who prefer the woman to carry the fetus to full term rather than carry out her decision to abort. Many men vow never to be in this predicament again. The emotions men feel, when faced with an abortion, are limitless. What is important to remember is that they do have genuine feelings and concerns about abortion that need to be expressed."[17]

It would appear then that men may experience many emotions after an abortion experience including anger, anxiety, grief, and guilt. They may be aware of these emotions at the time of the abortion or not until some time later. Whether a man is actually aware of his feelings or not, he may choose, consciously or unconsciously, to bury his feelings in order to maintain a strong, supportive front. In addition, men may feel confused about what to do and helpless in terms of how to support their partners.

Other researchers have studied the effects of abortion on the male-female relationship. The findings of their studies indicate that relationships may not survive the strain of an abortion experience. In one such study, 400 males were interviewed and the majority of them stated that they had been consulted about the abortion decision.[18] One month following the abortion, 70% of the relationships between these men and their partners had failed. In their book concerning men and abortion, Shostak and McLouth reported a 25% failure rate in relationships after abortion.[19] Still another study looked at the effects of abortion on the marriage relationship.[20] Some of the effects included: inability to conceive, emotional withdrawal, sexual and interpersonal conflicts, and a loss of trust. Vincent Rue, psychotherapist and co-director of the Institute for Pregnancy Loss, has suggested that the relationship problems experienced by some couples following an abortion may be due to the "basic inequality between the partners in the abortion decision."[21] He further states that because of this inequality, "the capacity to develop trust, communication and problem-solving skills, intimacy, honesty, and companionship is severely restricted."[22]

Men also may experience sexual dysfunction following abortion. In her book, *The Ambivalence of Abortion*, Linda Bird Francke describes several cases in which post-abortion men experienced impotency.[23] Some of the men I worked with also identified impotence as a problem. Furthermore, one of the men told me that the trauma of both abortion and his subsequent impotence led him into a homosexual relationship. He felt safer with a man after being hurt and humiliated by a woman. Eventually, this man ended the homosexual relationship because he knew he wanted to have a family. Berger has described a similar case in which a man who was hurt by his partner's insistence on abortion became actively involved in a homosexual lifestyle. The abortion occurred while the man was in his twenties and his homosexual involvement continued until he was in his mid-forties following psychotherapy.[24]

Another consequence of abortion may be the persistence of occasional thoughts about the fetus. Among 75 post-abortion men interviewed by Shostak and McLouth, less than one-third of the men reported having no thoughts about the fetus and 9% reported having frequent thoughts.[25] One of the men who volunteered to participate in our research was so plagued by persistent thoughts concerning his abortion experience that he was unable to concentrate. As a result, he was unable to hold down a job or remain in school. Another volunteer described recurrent dreams with themes of death. He clearly recognized the connection between his dreams and his abortion experience.

For those who are interested in reading more about the scientific study of men and abortion, I would recommend the book by Shostak and McLouth entitled *Men and Abortion: Lessons, Losses and Love.*[26] This work is the most comprehensive to date and involved a large sample of 1,000 men who were asked to complete a questionnaire while waiting in an abortion clinic. Data was gathered at 30 abortion clinics across the county. The authors then interviewed a subsample of 75 of the men either in person or by phone. However, I need to point out that these authors devote only five and one-half pages of their 333-page book to those men who were opposed to their partners' decisions to abort. These men were described as experiencing a very profound sense of personal loss. While those men who were opposed to the abortion comprised only 11% or 110 males of the total sample, this group may represent the population at large. If that is the case, then we can approximate the number of men who have been deeply hurt by abortion. Given the fact that there have been about 37 million abortions performed since its legalization, there may be more than 3 million men in this country alone who have been deeply traumatized by an abortion experience.

Based on the limited amount of information available at this time, it would seem that men may experience similar emotions to those of women after an abortion. These emotions may include anger, anxiety, grief, and guilt. In addition, men may feel helpless and suffer the break-up of a meaningful relationship following an abortion. The unequal power distribution concerning the abortion decision may intensify the man's suffering and contribute to a failed relationship. The men I have interviewed, who were opposed to their partners' decisions to abort, were truly devastated. They found themselves absolutely powerless to protect their unborn children. They are acutely aware of the inherent injustice in only one parent having the power to determine whether a child of two parents will live or die. Each of these men lost a relationship with a woman he loved, a child he desperately wanted to protect, and the hopes and dreams he had for the future. Finally, in spite of the blurring of gender roles, men are still under enormous pressure to contain emotion and maintain a strong front. This, too, may make the resolution of their abortion experience more difficult.

The personal stories included in this book have been contributed by men who have actually experienced abortion and suffered the painful consequences. These personal accounts may help others who have been hurt by an abortion to see that their responses are normal and that they are not alone.

Chapter Two

Post-Abortion Stress in Men

MEN MAY FIND THEMSELVES in a variety of situations which lead to the decision to end a pregnancy. These include the following:

1) Both the man and his female partner agree to obtain an abortion. There may be a great deal of or very little discussion prior to the abortion decision.
2) The man may pressure his partner to abort. He may do this directly or by threatening to leave the relationship if she does not choose abortion.
3) Someone else (such as a friend or parent) may pressure his partner to choose abortion. In such a case, the man may or may not have expressed his opinion about the decision.
4) The man may abandon the relationship in order to avoid the abortion decision entirely.
5) The man may remain in the relationship but passively

leave the abortion decision to his partner. His passivity may be due to his confusion about what to do or to his belief that it is her, and only her, decision to make.

6) His partner may chose abortion against his wishes. She may make this decision in spite of his protest and his offers to support her and the child.
7) The man may not know about the pregnancy or the abortion until some time after the abortion occurs.

Regardless of how the decision is made, any man who has had a personal abortion experience is at risk for developing symptoms of post-abortion stress. Dr. Vincent Rue has argued that men, as well as women, can suffer negative effects from abortion.[1] He states that "men, too, experience emotional problems following abortion."[2]

This chapter will enumerate the various problems that men may experience. These may be apparent immediately after the abortion decision is made or much later, even years after the abortion occurred.

Some men may experience various symptoms or problems and not realize that they are related to a past abortion. Other men may be very much aware that abortion is the cause of their pain.

The following is a list of the potential symptoms or problems that men may experience after abortion. The post-abortion man may use this as a checklist in order to determine if he is suffering from post-abortion stress. It is particularly significant if the man has experienced these symptoms only *after* his abortion experience. If that is the case, then it is more likely that the abortion is the source of his problems. (I have categorized the problems as relating to anger, helplessness, anxiety, relationships, guilt, and grief. However, in reality, many of these problems are not limited to a single category. For example, "worrying" may be related to both anxiety and guilt because when we feel guilty, we also tend to feel anxious.)

A. Problems related to ANGER
   ___frequent, angry outbursts
   ___violent behavior
   ___increased risk-taking behaviors (for example, driving recklessly)
   ___frequent feelings of anger toward the self
   ___frequent feelings of anger toward his partner or women in general

B. Problems related to HELPLESSNESS
   ___confusion about a man's role in society
   ___feeling inept or unable to function as a man (for example, some men may question whether they are able to support or nurture a family)

C. Problems related to ANXIETY
   ___difficulty sleeping
   ___disturbing dreams or nightmares
   ___difficulty concentrating
   ___excessive worrying

D. Problems related to RELATIONSHIPS
   ___isolation (either feeling alone or deliberately choosing to avoid people)
   ___fear of relationships
   ___promiscuity (many casual, sexual relationships with several partners)
   ___sexual problems (such as impotence)
   ___difficulty trusting women
   ___difficulty communicating with others, particularly with women

E. Problems related to GRIEF and/or GUILT
   ___frequent feelings of sadness
   ___frequent thoughts of self-condemnation, shame, or guilt
   ___frequent feelings of hopelessness
   ___persistent thoughts about the abortion and/or the baby
   ___increased feelings of sadness at certain times of the year (for example during the month the abortion occurred or the month when the baby would have been born)
   ___discomfort around or avoidance of babies and small children
   ___frequent crying spells
   ___a feeling of choking or tightness in the throat
   ___feeling numb or dead inside
   ___alcohol and/or drug abuse
   ___thoughts of suicide (Anyone experiencing thoughts of suicide should contact a professional counselor.)

All post-abortion men will not demonstrate all of these symptoms or problems. Some will experience more of them than other men. If a man checks several of these as part of his experience and if he believes that they may be related to a previous abortion, then it is important for him to work through his pain and to avoid the tendency to deny or repress his negative emotions. Also, he must be reassured that his feelings are normal in response to his significant loss.

Both men and women may choose to avoid dealing with negative emotions, but men may tend to deny or repress their emotions more so than women. This tendency may be due to a number of factors. One of these is the socialization process of men in our culture. Men are expected to contain emotion and put up a strong front. When they do so, they may be attempting to live up to society's expectations. Men also may avoid expressing negative emotions because they are genuinely concerned about supporting their partners. They may believe that expressing their own feelings would only cause more upset for their partners. Over and over, men have been bombarded with the message that abortion is the woman's choice and not his to make. So, in an attempt to 'do the right thing,' a man facing an unplanned pregnancy may keep his thoughts and feelings to himself. If he then becomes aware of anger and grief after the abortion, he will, unfortunately, often be confronted with society's lack of sympathy or even acknowledgment of his pain.

The repression of negative emotions (such as anger, helplessness, guilt, and grief) may feel better in the short run but will only result in complications down the road. Negative emotions that are not acknowledged and worked through have a life of their own and may surface at moments when we least expect them. This can be confusing to say the least.

Anger that is not expressed appropriately is likely to be expressed at inappropriate times or in future relationships. For example, a post-abortion man who has not dealt with his anger, may unconsciously direct that anger towards women in general, thus preventing him from having a meaningful relationship with any woman. Likewise, another man may become involved in a new relationship and, upon discovering that his new partner has an abortion in her past, he may displace his anger on to her. He may be conscious of or completely unaware of doing so.

If his feelings of helplessness are not faced, the post-abortion man may experience a severe lack of self-esteem or a lack of confidence in himself. This may be apparent not only in his relationships but also in his job performance or in his academic pursuits.

Unresolved guilt can contribute to fear and anxiety and may result in an inability to concentrate. His lack of concentration may make it difficult for him to finish projects or to study in school. Excessive guilt also may be manifest in self-destructive or self-punishing behaviors such as driving too fast, binge drinking, or drug abuse.

When grief is not processed or resolved, it may be referred to as complicated or pathological mourning. Grief that is not resolved can lead to depression. Grief, too, can surface when we least expect it. For example, a man who has an abortion in his past may become overwhelmed with grief the next time he impregnates a woman or when his first child is born. This reaction may be completely confusing to him or it may lead to a new awareness that his past abortion experience is causing his discomfort. One of the men I interviewed told me that during his wife's pregnancy (when he was expecting his first child to be born), he was consumed with fears that the child would not be healthy. He knew his fears weren't rational and realized that his guilt about a previous abortion was causing him to worry excessively.

Repressed emotions may not just affect us psychologically, but physically as well. A considerable amount of research has been done to investigate the potential effects of our emotions on our physical health. This area of study is referred to as health psychology. For the Christian man, there are also the spiritual consequences to consider when he denies or represses his emotions. His relationship with God may be affected and he may feel distant from God or question God's love for him.

Given the risks of choosing to avoid his pain, the post-abortion man would be wise to face his pain and to work through it. This may be done with the help of professional counselors, pastoral counselors, other post-abortion men and women who have found healing, Bible Studies written for post-abortion men, or, hopefully, reading a book such as this. When choosing an individual to share his pain with, it is essential that he choose someone who is empathetic and who believes that abortion can cause psychological pain and grief.

Regardless of the type of help he seeks, it is essential for the post-abortion man to be honest with himself about his feelings and his fears and to recognize that they are a normal response to his loss. I am convinced that if he chooses to actively work toward his healing, he will achieve it and he will experience renewed hope for his future.

The next two chapters discuss forgiveness as a means to find healing after a deep and unjust injury. Part Two of this book covers the most common emotional responses to abortion and also considers how these emotions can be dealt with.

Chapter Three

Forgiveness: A Psychological Model

GIVEN THE EVIDENCE THAT abortion can be a very traumatic experience for men, I decided to develop a program that I believed could be beneficial to post-abortion men. With Dr. Robert Enright, professor and psychologist, I designed a clinical intervention study in order to test the efficacy of this program.[1] The goal of the program was to help the men work towards forgiveness. Each man was asked to identify one person, other than himself, whom he most blamed for the abortion. He was also asked if he, himself, felt guilt or responsibility. We then worked toward forgiving the identified other as well as on self-forgiveness when appropriate.

Readers who are interested in a description of the actual research may read more about it in Appendix A. The rest of this chapter will describe the psychological model of forgiveness on which the intervention program was based. Part Two of this book will follow the actual intervention program as it was utilized with the men who participated in the research.

As I write this chapter, I am curious as to the reader's thoughts and reactions to the topic of forgiveness. I remember working with one of my first volunteers. When I initially told him that the goal of the intervention program was forgiveness, he said, rather loudly, "What?! You mean I'm supposed to forgive someone for murder?" His reaction is not unusual given the pain he was feeling and the fact that people may confuse forgiving with excusing, pardoning, forgetting, or reconciliation. Genuine forgiveness is none of these and will be contrasted with each of these forms of pseudoforgiveness.

When one is excused for his or her wrongdoing, the one who does the excusing must have a rational reason for deciding that the offender cannot be held responsible. For example, if I am hit by a car and I suffer permanent physical damage, I will probably blame the driver of the car. If I later find out that the manufacturer of the car installed defective brakes, I may excuse the driver and blame the manufacturer. The driver can't reasonably be held accountable for the failure of the brakes. In this case, the driver is excused and there is no point in my forgiving him since he is not responsible.

To offer pardon to someone who has offended us is to release the offender from legal penalties. However, we may forgive someone for a criminal injury even while our judicial system enforces its penalties. Going back to the previous example, imagine that the person who hit me with his car was drunk while driving. I may be able to genuinely forgive him for my physical injuries and for my suffering. Yet, I decide not to testify in his behalf in a court of law. The driver is eventually tried, found guilty, and sentenced.

Forgiveness is also not to be confused with forgetting. We humans aren't designed to forget. It is through memory that we store information and learn. The fact that we can remember that which has caused us pain helps us to avoid being hurt in the future. When we are deeply and unfairly hurt by another, we don't forget. In fact, we may find ourselves thinking about the injury over and over. Lewis Smedes has written a book entitled, *Forgive and Forget: Healing the Hurts We Don't Deserve.*[2] Smedes wisely observes that "forgetting, in fact, may be a dangerous way to escape the inner surgery of the heart that we call forgiving." To say "forgiving isn't easy" would be a gross understatement. It is truly a demanding and difficult work of the heart.

Finally, forgiveness is not reconciliation. We can forgive someone and decide not to stay in a relationship with that person. For example, if a woman is being physically abused by her husband, she may be able to offer him genuine forgiveness. However, it may not be in her (or her husband's and children's) best interest to remain in a close relationship with him. Reconciliation depends on trust. We may forgive others and still not trust them. Forgiving doesn't mean that we have to become martyrs or doormats for those who have harmed us.

So what exactly is forgiveness? It is the conscious decision to withhold both retribution and resentment and to instead offer mercy to the undeserving offender. According to philosopher, Joanna North, genuine forgiveness occurs when the injured party chooses to "view the wrongdoer with compassion, benevolence, and love while recognizing that he has willfully abandoned them."[3] When forgiveness is genuine, it is a gift offered willingly and without condition. Reconciliation may be conditional but genuine forgiveness is not.

Genuine forgiveness may occur without any apology or even recognition of wrongdoing on the part of the offender. "Forgiveness is an internal process that transforms the forgiver and also may transform the one forgiven, if the offender is able to receive forgiveness as a gift."[4] Some of those who have hurt us deeply have since died. I would argue that it is still possible for us to forgive them. Others who have hurt us may refuse to accept any responsibility for the injury. Therefore, they do not see themselves as in need of receiving forgiveness. Nonetheless, we can still choose to forgive them and reap the benefits of that choice. In the ideal situation, the offender would recognize her need for forgiveness and would be willing to receive it. In such a case, both the offender and the injured could experience the healing that forgiveness brings.

Dr. Enright and the Human Development Study Group at the University of Wisconsin-Madison have developed a process model of interpersonal forgiveness that may be reviewed in Appendix B.[5] This model integrates the thinking, feeling, and behavioral aspects of the forgiveness process. The model consists of twenty units. These are referred to as "psychological variables" and we realize that we don't move through them in a fixed step-like order. Instead, when we are working on forgiving another, we tend to move back and forth among the units until we finally complete the forgiveness journey. Everyone will work through these units in a different order and, as they do so, will experience different degrees of difficulty. Some people may even skip over some of the steps or units. The model and each unit will be described in terms of how they could be applied to a post-abortion man.

The man who is carrying pain due to a past abortion may experience healing through forgiveness. Before he can begin the process of forgiveness, he must determine whom he blames for the abortion. It may be that he blames himself as well as another in which case both self-forgiveness and forgiveness of the other may be beneficial. While the focus of this chapter is on interpersonal forgiveness, or forgiving another, the process of self-forgiveness is quite similar and will be discussed in Chapter 7.

Uncovering Phase

The first step or unit requires that the post-abortion man examine the defense mechanisms he has used to protect himself from pain (unit 1). Of course, men who have fallen into patterns of denial will not be aware of having done so. That is the very nature of denial. Men in denial may feel sadness or anxiety and not be aware of the source of these emotions. They may engage in risky or self-destructive behaviors and not see an association between the abortion and their behavior. It is possible that, at some time in the future, an event will break the denial. For instance, when a post-abortion man actually has a child, he may finally realize the impact of his previous abortion experience. I would encourage a man with an abortion in his past to at least consider the possibility that he has deliberately avoided acknowledging a significant injury due to the abortion. Furthermore, he might consider if his current thoughts, feelings, and behaviors are related to a past abortion experience.

If the man concludes that he has been deeply hurt by abortion, he may become aware of feeling intense anger toward the one(s) he blames for his abortion experience (2). In addition, he may become aware of feeling shame and/or guilt (3). This is especially likely if he, even passively, supported the abortion decision.

As the post-abortion man becomes increasingly aware of his negative emotions, he also may become aware of "cathexis" (4). Cathexis is a psychoanalytic term which refers to the positive or negative emotional attachment a person has to a person, object, or event. For the post-abortion man, there may be considerable emotional attachment to the abortion and/or his partner.

As he continues to explore his responses to the injury, he may realize that he frequently relives the hurtful abortion experience in his mind (5). This is referred to as "cognitive rehearsal." Recurrent thoughts of the abortion experience may interfere with his ability to concentrate and may perpetuate negative feelings such as anger, sadness, helplessness, fear, and/or guilt. The post-abortion man also may feel resentful if he perceives the one who hurt him to be in a better state than he is (6). For example, he may perceive his partner to be relatively pain-free or he may view the doctor who performed the abortion as being rewarded for hurting another.

A man who has been hurt by abortion may conclude that he has been permanently and adversely changed by his experience (7). Abortion is, after all, permanent. It cannot be undone. He also may find himself struggling with issues of justice if he experienced helplessness in his attempts to exert any legal or social pressure in opposing the abortion (8).

These first eight steps or variables comprise the "uncovering" phase of the forgiveness process. During this phase, the injured man is discovering much about himself in terms of both his response to the injury and the effects of the injury on himself.

Decision Phase

This increasing awareness of his response to and the consequences of the abortion is not a pleasant awakening. Rather, the man may feel quite miserable and in need of relief. He may realize that something must change in order for him to at least get a grip on himself and his life (9). While there may be a temptation to repress his uncomfortable feelings, repression will not bring him long-term relief. In fact, such a choice will only waste psychological energy which could be used more productively.

Instead, I would ask the post-abortion man to at least consider forgiveness as an option which may enable him to work through his pain and loss (10). Forgiveness is more likely to bring resolution than other options such as repression, letting go, avoidance by keeping busy, or trying to talk himself out of the fact that he was deeply hurt. Each of these other options was put into practice by one or more of the men who participated in our research. None of them provided long-term relief or resolution. On the other hand, as these men worked toward and actually came to forgive the ones who hurt them, they benefited from significant decreases in their levels of anger, anxiety, and grief. With these favorable results in mind, I would encourage the post-abortion man to make a commitment to forgive the one who has harmed him (11). The decision to work towards forgiveness is a critical step. It is a turning point. Such a decision signifies a desire to heal, to offer healing to another, and hope that healing is possible.

Units 9 through 11 are together referred to as the "decision" phase. While the decision to forgive is a critical turning point in the process, there is still a good deal of work required in order to actually carry out the commitment to forgive.

Work Phase

The working phase of the forgiveness process requires that the man engage in reframing (12) his experience so as to develop empathy toward his offender (and himself if he is struggling with self-forgiveness). Reframing is a deliberate and conscious attempt to view the one who hurt us in as large a context as possible. The post-abortion man may begin to reframe by considering the immediate context of his offender at the time of the abortion. This would include personality factors, family and societal pressures, and any other stressors that the offender was dealing with. Next, the man might enlarge this context as fully as possible by considering the fact that the one who hurt him is a fellow human being. If the man believes that his unborn child had inherent worth as a person, I would challenge him to view his offender as having inherent worth too. One of our research volunteers, when speaking about this notion of inherent worth, stated that "there is something good about everyone... there's potential for all of us to go either way." He was saying that each of us, as human beings, has the potential to engage in either good or bad behavior. He believed that this capacity to choose good or evil gives the individual inherent worth. Other post-abortion men may accept the premise of every human being having inherent worth as part of their religious beliefs. In such a case, I would suggest that it is only logical for them to apply that belief to their offenders (and themselves in terms of self-forgiveness).

Reframing also may be facilitated by reminding the man that a single act does not define the individual. Parents are quite cognizant of this fact. In order for them to effectively discipline their children, they must be able to separate bad behavior from the children themselves and also to take into account the developmental level of their children. A post-abortion man who has parented a child may easily relate to this point that children must be disciplined for bad behavior but accepted as valuable people in spite of their behavior. When parents make such a distinction, they are reframing. They are seeing their children as having worth even as they behave in an unworthy manner. Parents who take into account their children's development are also reframing. They use realistic expectations based on the child's age and experience to determine the child's degree of responsibility. Granted, this parent-child analogy has some limitations. Assuming the post-abortion man and woman are adults, discipline of one by the other may not seem appropriate. Nonetheless, the ability to separate an individual's actions from his/her worth is essential in both successful parenting and successful forgiveness.

As the man enlarges the frame through which he views the one who hurt him, he may come to see the larger context surrounding her behavior. As he views the big picture, it becomes easier for him to understand why she behaved as she did. In my work with post-abortion men, I found this particular unit of the forgiveness process to be very challenging. I believe there are two factors which can make this step difficult. First, there may be some confusion regarding the purpose of reframing. I want to stress that the singular purpose of reframing is to increase our understanding of another's behavior and NOT to excuse that behavior. If a person's behavior were excusable, there would be nothing to forgive. Second, it is often easier to change our thoughts toward those who have hurt us than it is to change our feelings toward them. This phenomenon was apparent in a large scale study of U.S. college students and their parents.[6]

The ability to reframe, which is a cognitive or thinking exercise, is critical in order to develop the positive feelings of empathy and compassion toward one who has hurt us (13 & 14). Empathy is a vicarious emotion which allows one to imagine and understand how another thinks and/or feels. Empathy also allows an injured person to appreciate the suffering of the one who injured him. The appreciation of another's suffering can, in turn, enable the forgiver to feel compassion toward the one who has injured him. Compassion may be thought of as an attitude of tender mercy.

In addition to their fear and anxiety upon discovering that they are unexpectedly pregnant, many women have suffered from their decisions to abort. Evidence concerning the negative effects of abortion for women has been documented.[7,8] Even as a man may struggle with post-abortion pain, so too may his partner. Both may believe that they have suffered a traumatic loss. One of our research volunteers said this about his suffering, "The suffering increased my capacity for empathy for someone in a similar situation." A post-abortion man may find it easier to empathize and feel compassion for the partner who hurt him if he considers the possibility that she may be bearing grief just as he is. If his partner shows no evidence of remorse and he believes she has not been hurt, he might keep in mind the fact that some women may cope by using denial or by expressing disdain toward those who would deny women the 'right to abortion.' Women may choose these means of coping rather than facing the nagging inner doubts and guilt about their decisions. Some women, who initially appear relieved since the immediate problem (i.e. pregnancy) has been removed, may not exhibit symptoms of what has come to be called "Post-Abortion Syndrome"[9] until months or even years later. Even if a female partner appears to be unaffected by the abortion, she is at risk for future pain simply because of the choice she made.

I want to stress once again that there is no place for excuse-making in the forgiveness process. The purpose of reframing is to develop empathy and compassion toward one who has hurt us but is never to be used to excuse or condone what the offender has done. Forgiveness does not demand that we ignore justice. In fact, we must have an adequate sense of justice in order to recognize when we have been treated unfairly. Forgiveness involves both the recognition that an injustice occurred and a decision to respond to that injustice with mercy. It is, in effect, the giving of a moral gift to an undeserving person.

Forgiveness may be thought of as moral because it entails giving up feelings, thoughts, and behaviors that demonstrate ill will and replacing them with feelings, thoughts, and behaviors that demonstrate goodwill toward the offender. Forgiveness may be thought of as a gift because it is a generous and unmerited response to one who does not deserve such a gift.

The defining feature of the "gift" of forgiveness may be seen in unit 15 of the forgiveness process, the "acceptance/absorption of pain." This step refers to the conscious decision, on the part of the injured, to not only accept the pain which he has suffered but also to avoid passing it on to innocent others. One of the men in our study likened this idea to the process of phagocytosis in which the white cells of our bloodstream engulf invading bacteria to prevent them from further attack. When we make a conscious effort to absorb the pain of an injury, we are taking the first step to preventing ourselves from passing that pain onto others or as the research volunteer put it, we are "reducing the spill area."

The process of phagocytosis is an automatic process in a healthy body. The absorption of psychological pain following a deep hurt is not an automatic process. It requires an act of will on the part of the man to deliberately avoid inflicting his suffering on both the one who hurt him and on other innocent people. This then is the gift he is giving to an undeserving recipient. Having been grossly wronged, he has a right to retaliate and to mete out justice. Instead, as he forgives, he chooses to control his pain and aggression and to behave mercifully.

This is not to say the post-abortion man should not share his pain with an empathetic listener. He may find a good deal of relief by speaking with another trusted person about his experience. Simply talking about the experience should result in a decrease of negative emotions. It is the residual or left-over pain that needs to be controlled. If the post-abortion man can say to himself, "I can't undo the hurt but I can try to not let my pain hurt others," he will not only avoid retaliatory behavior, but he will avoid intensifying his injury by incurring more guilt and remorse.

Professor of psychology, Allen Bergin, suggests that the "absorption of pain" entailed in true forgiveness also prevents "the process of transmitting pain from generation to generation."[10] In a sense then, forgiveness may not only benefit current relationships, but future ones as well.

Deepening Phase

A post-abortion man may well ask why he has been treated unfairly particularly by a partner he loved and thought he could trust. It is natural for us to wonder why bad things happen and why people hurt us. The problem with this question is that we frequently don't find a satisfactory answer. I would not try to dissuade a man from courteously confronting his partner with the question, "Why?" However, I would warn him that he may not get an answer he is hoping for or that helps him to heal. What he can do is to try to find meaning in his suffering (16). This may be accomplished by thinking about what he has or could learn from his hurtful experience. Several of our research participants said that they learned a lot about what was important to them and what they really wanted in life. Others stated that their suffering taught them about both their limits and their abilities. None of them would describe their abortion experience as valuable but each of them could describe a valuable lesson that came with the experience.

As the post-abortion man continues on his forgiveness journey, it may be helpful for him to realize that he has also needed to be forgiven (17). While he may not be responsible for the abortion and subsequent pain, he has been responsible for hurting others in the past. We have all hurt people and needed to receive their forgiveness. We have all been deeply wounded by others and they have needed to receive forgiveness from us. The insight that he is not alone in either his suffering or his struggle to forgive (18) may comfort the post-abortion man and reinforce his decision to forgive.

The man may discover a new purpose in life because of his injury (19). It is my impression that finding meaning and finding a new purpose in life are very related. For some post-abortion men, the discovery of a new purpose, such as helping other men who have been hurt by abortion, comes first. This new purpose is what gives their abortion experience meaning. Other men may first find meaning in their experience and then be motivated to use their newfound knowledge to help other people. Regardless of which comes first, finding meaning or finding a new purpose, both of these help to make the post-abortion man feel more hopeful and less helpless.

The post-abortion man who completes the forgiveness journey is rewarded with, at the very least, a decrease in negative thoughts and emotions (20). I have observed that a man who has been hurt by the abortion decision of his partner may first notice a change in his thoughts toward her. His thoughts become more positive and he is able to wish her well even if he still feels some anger towards her. After this, he begins to be aware of feeling more positively as well. His anger lessens and he feels genuine compassion for her. Some of the men in our study even demonstrated positive behaviors toward the women who hurt them. One gave his former partner a Christmas gift and told her that he had forgiven her. Another called his former partner and gave her the opportunity to share her pain regarding the abortion. After realizing the benefits of sharing his pain with an empathetic listener, he wanted to give her the same opportunity. His compassionate feeling was demonstrated in his behavior.

I am not suggesting that a man hasn't forgiven if he can't yet reach out with a positive gesture toward the one who hurt him. The post-abortion man has forgiven when he decides to withhold punishment from the one who hurt him and to entertain kinder thoughts toward her. The gift of forgiveness may be large or small. The generosity of the gift may vary depending on the person and the injury.

Dr. Enright has described the gift-giving nature of forgiveness as a paradox.[11] He points out that when the forgiver gives up his justified resentment and his right to retaliate, he is giving the offender a gift she doesn't deserve and, as he does so, he receives a gift himself, the gift of healing.

So, forgiveness benefits both the forgiver and the one forgiven. The forgiver obtains an improved emotional state and regains a feeling of control over himself. This may lead to other improvements such as increased hope and self-esteem. The person forgiven will only experience the healing power of forgiveness if she recognizes her need for and is able to accept forgiveness. In such a case, she will benefit from knowing that she doesn't have to fear punishment and that she has regained the respect of the one she injured.

Of course, there will be times when the offender doesn't believe that she has done anything wrong. In that case, she can't receive the gift offered to her. She also may have difficulty accepting the gift if she is actively condemning herself and feels unworthy to receive it. In this case, time and repeated offers of forgiveness may eventually help her to receive forgiveness.

The positive changes in the forgiver's thoughts, feelings, and behavior may pave the way to reconciliation. However, forgiveness does not guarantee reconciliation. We can genuinely forgive those who have hurt us and still choose not to remain in relationships with them. This may be necessary when the offender cannot be trusted to stop hurting us.

Remember, the forgiveness process does not occur in neat and tidy steps and stages. When we embark on the journey of forgiveness, we often find ourselves reworking some problems we thought we had finished dealing with. It is quite possible for an individual to make the decision to forgive only to find himself feeling somewhat angry the next time he has contact with the one who hurt him. This doesn't mean that he hasn't made any progress, only that there is still progress to be made.

I believe that forgiveness brings more closure than other responses to deep and unjust hurt. Although forgiveness requires a good deal of work, it is, in the long run, less difficult than denial or repression. Forgiveness also fosters peace because it is motivated by compassion and requires the injured to control the expression of his pain. Furthermore, forgiveness is a response that one can be proud of. There is no shame in offering mercy to one who doesn't deserve it. It is not evidence of weakness or ignorance. The forgiver doesn't have to throw away his self-respect and sense of justice. Instead, the choice to forgive indicates a courageous willingness to take a risk.

Following this chapter, there is a case study based on the actual experience of one of our research participants. This case study, "Matthew's Story," will serve to clarify the process of forgiveness as it has been described in this chapter. The steps of the forgiveness process, as described in the case study, are indicated in parentheses.

Matthew's Story

MATTHEW, A YOUNG professional man in his early twenties, experienced an abortion during his college years. His girlfriend became pregnant and they decided to marry. Soon after this decision, his girlfriend informed him that she had changed her mind and had scheduled an abortion. Matthew was devastated. He tried to persuade her to continue the pregnancy even if she didn't want to marry him. He offered her financial and emotional support and begged to be given custody of the child. His girlfriend refused and went ahead with the abortion. Their relationship ended and the next time Matthew attempted physical intimacy with a woman, he suffered impotence. Matthew believed that this was due to his fear of pregnancy and having to endure a second abortion. Not long after, Matthew became involved in a homosexual relationship. He stated that he "felt safer with another man" after his hurtful experiences with females. Eventually, he left this relationship because he "wanted to have a family." When I met Matthew, he was engaged to a woman and he explained that he wanted to deal with the emotional problems he was still experiencing since the abortion. He hoped that he could find some resolution of old business in order to avoid having it affect his current relationship.

Matthew was quite able to express his anger and very much aware of the emotional energy attached to his memories (Steps 2 & 4). He was also aware of what triggered mental rehearsal of the abortion experience (5). For example, he stated that "radical feminists" made him angry when they referred to abortion as a woman's right "because men have rights too." He became so angry after watching a dramatic television program in which abortion was a major theme that he "had to leave the room." As we discussed how his anger was influencing current relationships, Matthew agreed that he needed some new strategies to deal with his anger (9).

When I first mentioned forgiveness to Matthew, he said, "What? You mean I'm supposed to forgive someone for murder?!" After clarifying forgiveness versus excusing, Matthew became receptive to the idea of forgiving his former partner and eventually committed himself to working towards forgiveness (10 & 11). We spent a good deal of time discussing what his girlfriend had been like and were able to reframe his experience in light of this discussion (12). Matthew remembered that she had been extremely concerned with "letting her parents down" and felt a great need to live up to perceived expectations. We also discussed the societal pressures on women today. Eventually Matthew was able to empathize and express compassion toward her (13 & 14).

Matthew also came to understand the concept of "absorbing the pain" (15). He demonstrated this in his comments concerning some abuse and neglect he had endured as a child. He told me that he didn't want to ever repeat what he had been through as a child and that he had made a conscious decision to avoid passing his pain on to his future children and to treat them kindly. It seemed very important to Matthew to create the family he never had and to be a loving father.

While Matthew did not describe himself as religious, he did describe himself as "very spiritual." He came to see his decision to forgive as perhaps good for all, in the sense that each of our decisions affect the entire community around us. This view seemed to give him a sense of meaning and of hope (16).

Matthew also recognized that he was not alone in his suffering (18) and that, because of his painful experience, he was well qualified to relate to other post-abortion men (19).

At our last meeting, Matthew was considerably more relaxed and able to laugh than when I first met him. He was looking forward to his upcoming marriage and the possibility of a family. While he still struggled with negative emotions in response to certain triggers, he was hopeful and confident that he could now have a healthy relationship with a woman. His commitment to forgive the one who hurt him brought him both hope and healing.

Chapter Four

FORGIVENESS: A CHRISTIAN IMPERATIVE

A PSYCHOLOGICAL MODEL can be very useful in explaining 'how' one goes about forgiving. However, for those who believe in Christ, forgiveness is much more than a mere psychological construct. It is rather the core of the Christian faith. It is both the gift that saves us from our sins and the gift that we are commanded to give to those who sin against us. In this chapter, I would like to briefly discuss the Christian concept of forgiveness and then compare that concept with the psychological model previously described.

For the Christian, the gospel or "good news" is the promise of God's forgiveness and accompanying salvation. The forgiveness of sins is promised to all who believe in Christ's divinity and atoning death on the cross. The prophets of the Old Testament foretold of Christ's coming and His suffering for our sins. The New Testament further describes the conditions which must be met to receive God's gift of forgiveness.

First, one must believe in Jesus Christ. After all, we cannot receive a gift from one we don't believe exists. In the New Testament book of Acts, we read that "All the prophets testify about Him that everyone who believes in Him receives forgiveness of sins through His name."[1] In the book of Romans, the apostle Paul states that, "This righteousness from God comes through faith in Jesus Christ to all who believe."[2] Thus, one must have faith that Christ exists in order to receive forgiveness or anything else from Him.

Paul goes on to write, "For all have sinned and fall short of the glory of God."[3] This implies a second condition to receiving God's forgiveness, that is, a recognition of our sinful nature. Unless we see ourselves as guilty, we aren't going to recognize our need to repent and be forgiven.

Finally, the Christian is commanded to forgive those who sin against him. Perhaps the most familiar reference to this command is contained within the Lord's prayer: "...forgive us our sins for we also forgive everyone who sins against us."[4] Jesus stated this more forcefully saying, "And when you stand praying, if you hold anything against anyone, forgive him, so that your Father in heaven may forgive you."[5] His command is reiterated in the book of Matthew, "For if you forgive men when they sin against you, your heavenly Father will also forgive you. But if you do not forgive men their sins, your Father will not forgive your sins."[6]

God's forgiveness of us is described in Scripture as conditional. However, God's command that we forgive those who sin against us is to be *unconditional*. Our forgiveness of others is to be unconditional because Christ has already paid the price for both our sins and the sins of those who sin against us. Thus, the act of forgiving those who wrong us is clearly an imperative for those of us who call ourselves Christians. While the previously described model of interpersonal forgiveness was not developed as a 'Christian' model, it is certainly not incompatible with this Christian imperative.

Looking first at unit 1 of the model, "examination of psychological defenses," I believe it is safe to say that all people, regardless of their religious beliefs, will employ various defense mechanisms when they feel threatened. One might reasonably speculate that Christians may be even more likely than others to engage in denial if they believe that their negative emotions are sinful. Therefore, the Christian, as well as the non-Christian, would do well to consider that he may be in denial regarding the effects of a sin, such as abortion, committed against him or by him.

The second unit of the psychological model has to do with confronting one's anger and releasing it in an appropriate way. Christians are not immune to negative emotions. The very fact that Scripture contains instructions regarding how to deal with anger confirms that the Christian is vulnerable to this emotion. In Paul's letter to the church at Ephesus, he says,"In your anger, do not sin."[7] There is no condemnation for the experience of anger and no prohibition against the expression of anger. The reader is simply told not to allow his anger to lead to sinful behavior. Jesus said, "If your brother sins against you, go and show him his fault, just between the two of you."[8] It is apparent, then, that the Christian has permission to confront his offender. However, the apostle John reminds the believers, "This is the message that you heard from the beginning: We should love one another."[9] So, while the Christian is permitted to confront, he is expected to do so with love.

Unit 3 of the model pertains to the admittance of shame when appropriate. We also may feel guilty if we contributed to the injury in any way. Shame and guilt are not exactly the same. Shame is similar to embarrassment. Sometimes an injury done to us by another may cause us to feel ashamed particularly if the injury resulted in public humiliation. Guilt, on the other hand, is felt when we recognize our own sin or failing. Again, it should be obvious that the Christian is not immune to such feelings. A Christian man who has experienced an unwanted abortion may feel ashamed that he trusted his partner and she betrayed him. He may feel guilty for being in a sexual relationship with a woman he was not married to or for encouraging her to have an abortion.

Like his non-Christian counterpart, the Christian post-abortion man may find himself caught up in an unhealthy pattern of ruminating over the abortion (unit 5) and, as he does so, he may make unfavorable comparisons between himself and the one who hurt him (6). As he realizes the degree to which he has been permanently changed by the abortion experience (7), he may question the 'fairness' of life in general (8). These experiences are common to both the Christian and the non-Christian. Such thoughts may perpetuate and exacerbate his anger and resentment.

Given the scriptural admonitions to both control one's anger and to forgive, one would hope that the Christian, in the decision phase of the process (units 9-11), would be very much aware of his precarious situation and quite willing to forgive his offender. This decision to forgive may begin merely as an attempt to comply with scriptural admonition. There is nothing wrong with choosing to forgive out of obedience to the Lord's teachings. Jesus, Himself, declared that, "If you love me, you will obey what I command."[10] The apostle John made the following claim, "And this is love: that we walk in obedience to His commands."[11] While the initial motivation of seeking to obey is not in and of itself problematic, it will not be enough to carry the Christian to the point of actually forgiving. Like the non-Christian, he will have to actively work through his pain and the process of forgiveness.

He will first have to engage in reframing by viewing the one who hurt him in context (12). Besides considering the immediate circumstances surrounding the one who hurt him, he needs to recognize that, like himself, she is created and loved by God. In the gospel of John, Jesus states, "For God so loved the world that He gave His one and only Son, that whoever believes in Him shall not perish but have eternal life."[12] The 'world' includes all who live in it and Jesus' use of the word "whoever" needs no further explanation. In the gospel according to Matthew, one finds further assurance of the worth of all God's children as Jesus asks, "Are not two sparrows sold for a penny? Yet not one of them will fall to the ground apart from the will of your Father. And even the very hairs of your head are all numbered. So don't be afraid; you are worth more than many sparrows."[13] This recognition of the individual worth of all people provides the Christian with the largest of contexts in which to view and consider his offender more favorably. Rather than limiting his view of the one who hurt him through the frame of the injury, he is able to view her as a beloved creation of God. Again, reframing is not to be confused with excusing. Nowhere in Scripture is the Christian commanded to condone or excuse a hurtful and unjust act but he is commanded to "Be merciful, just as your Father is merciful."[14]

As the Christian comes to see his offender as a worthy but fallible human being, he may begin to experience empathy and compassion toward her (13 & 14). What began as Christian obligation or obedience may now become mature Christian forgiveness as described by the apostle Paul, "Be kind and compassionate to one another, forgiving each other, just as in Christ God forgave you."[15] Christian forgiveness demands an element of compassion. It is not enough to say the words and not experience the love of Christ.

In addition, the Christian must make a conscious decision to bear the pain (15) he has suffered. This is not to say he shouldn't share his grief and sadness by speaking with trusted loved ones or a professional counselor, but rather that he control the angry expression of pain that could hurt others. The Christian is instructed to "Be completely humble and gentle; be patient, bearing with one another in love."[16] As he attempts to do so, he may rely on the promise that God "daily bears our burdens."[17] Whatever pain remains after working through the forgiveness process will not be carried alone but with the help and strength of the Lord. Prayer may be especially beneficial in terms of seeking the Lord's help in the bearing of one's pain.

After the prostitute anointed Jesus' feet with her tears, He pointed out that the love she demonstrated toward Him was evidence of the forgiveness she had received. He then stated, "He who has been forgiven little loves little."[18] The Christian who recognizes that God has given him the undeserved gift of forgiveness should be ready to offer such a gift to one who has harmed him. How better to share the gospel than to demonstrate the love and mercy of Christ through the gift of interpersonal forgiveness?

As the Christian moves into the deepening phase of the forgiveness process, he also may be assured of finding meaning in his suffering (16). Paul's letter to the church in

Rome states, "And we know that in all things God works for the good of those who love Him."[19] Paul is not saying that everything that happens to the believer is good but rather that God will bring something good out of even the most unpleasant events. The mature Christian knows that spiritual growth and wisdom often follow painful life experiences. He is also aware of and humbled by his offenses against other people and recognizes his need to receive forgiveness from them (17). This recognition helps him to identify with and to appreciate the need of the one who hurt him. "For all have sinned and fall short of the glory of God,"[20] and he is not alone in this universal struggle (18).

As the Christian willingly shares the gift of forgiveness and experiences God's peace, he may come to recognize a new purpose in his life (19). For God "comforts us in all our troubles, so that we can comfort those in any trouble with the comfort we ourselves have received from God."[21] Our painful experiences can teach us much about suffering, forgiveness, and compassion. The Christian who works through his pain and genuinely forgives another is well-equipped to minister to others dealing with similar injuries.

Finally, as he completes the forgiveness journey, he becomes aware of a lightening of his burdens (i.e. a decrease in painful emotions) and an increase in genuine goodwill toward the one who offended him (20). His forgiveness may be further demonstrated in a genuine desire to pray for his offender or in good deeds toward her. As he willingly offers the healing gift of forgiveness to another, he himself experiences healing. As he forgives, or sets his offender free, he frees himself from anger, bitterness, and the subtle control of another.

The one forgiven also receives healing. In Paul's letter to the church in Corinth, he instructs the believers to forgive an offender "so that he will not be overwhelmed by excessive sorrow."[22] An offender who is able to receive the gift of forgiveness benefits from a reduction in sadness and the restoration of joy.

While forgiveness is essential in paving the way toward reconciliation, it cannot guarantee it. Ultimately, reconciliation will depend on the offender's recognition of wrongdoing, her willingness to receive forgiveness, and the degree of trust between the two individuals. However, even if reconciliation is not achieved, forgiveness opens the door to reconciliation and it brings an element of peace because the desire for retaliation has been relinquished and replaced with a desire for mercy. The act of forgiveness is the epitome of Christ-like behavior demonstrating His love and His mercy.

I have attempted to demonstrate that the psychological model described in the previous chapter is not incompatible with the Christian faith. However, there are some unique characteristics that the Christian brings to the forgiveness process. First and foremost is the Christian imperative to forgive. Forgiveness is not merely one of many responses the believer may choose from. It is the only acceptable response and one that provides the Christian with the continual assurance of God's salvation. Second, the Christian has God's own promise that He will empower the believer to carry out his decision to forgive. God will honor the decision to forgive by enabling the forgiver to experience a change of heart toward his offender and by helping to bear the pain the forgiver has suffered. Thus, while the believer is commanded to forgive (something quite contrary to his human nature), he is also promised God's help in order to do so.

Chris' Story

CHRIS WAS IN COLLEGE at a large public university when his girlfriend became pregnant. This was the first intimate relationship for both Chris and his partner. His initial reaction upon learning of his girlfriend's pregnancy was shock and fear. Both he and his partner, Angie, had been raised in Christian homes.

Soon after the shock wore off, Chris described himself as feeling ashamed and guilty about having a sexual relationship outside of marriage. He was concerned that this might prevent him from realizing his goal to become a youth pastor. At the same time, he believed strongly that abortion was morally wrong and he shared this belief with Angie.

Her response was firm; she would not consider any alternative but abortion. She did not want to marry Chris and did not believe that she could raise a child by herself. Chris begged her to reconsider and agreed to support the child and quit school if that was necessary. Ultimately, Angie had an abortion and the relationship ended a few months later.

When I met Chris, he was struggling with guilt and anger. He was feeling quite guilty about violating God's directions concerning relationships and he was also feeling angry at Angie for refusing to acknowledge his wishes and for ignoring the teachings of both his, and her, Christian upbringing.

Chris believed that God had forgiven him. In spite of that belief, he still struggled with self-forgiveness and with anger towards Angie. He was well aware that being a Christian did not make him immune to negative emotions but he also knew that his anger was interfering with both his relationship with God and with Angie.

He didn't need to be convinced that forgiving Angie was the right or moral thing to do. That was already an essential part of his Christian faith and he genuinely wanted to be obedient to God's teachings. While Chris had completed the decision phase of the forgiveness process, he needed some help in moving through the work phase.

With a bit of encouragement, Chris was able to reframe his views of both Angie and himself. He stated, "I realized the mistakes I've made in my life and the things I've done out of total ignorance so I certainly can't hold onto hostility and bitterness toward her." When he honestly recognized his own sins and failures, he became more empathetic toward Angie. He recognized that Angie was a vulnerable and fallible human being just as he was but that nonetheless, both were created and loved by God. He came to fully perceive how Angie's fear and embarrassment contributed to her decision. Chris was not excusing Angie; he was understanding the situation from her perspective and, as he did so, he began to feel genuine compassion toward her.

As Chris developed compassion and mercy toward this woman who had hurt him so deeply, I suggested he consider if God would not want him to be more merciful to himself as well. We spent a good deal of time talking about God's gift of forgiveness and our need to receive it. Specifically, I pointed out to him that our inability or unwillingness to receive such a gift must be very hurtful to God especially considering the cost. Chris had two choices. He could continue to condemn himself in spite of the fact that God no longer condemned him or he could choose to fully embrace God's gift. By choosing the latter, Chris opened himself up to self-forgiveness as well. He stopped condemning himself and trusted God to bring something good out of a very painful situation.

Chris became more optimistic about continuing to pursue his desire to become a youth minister. He realized that his experience could be of benefit to the adolescents that he hoped to work with. His experience would give credibility to his advice to them concerning both sexual relationships outside of marriage and the power of giving and receiving forgiveness. While he would always feel some sadness about his loss, Chris trusted God to help him to carry his grief.

Chris also was able to tell Angie that he had forgiven her. He continues to pray for her in the hope that she too will come to fully appreciate the healing that forgiveness brings.

Part Two:

Healing After Abortion

Jack's Story

JACK AND ERICA HAD BEEN dating seriously for about six months. They found out that Erica was pregnant very early on in her pregnancy and were excited about the prospect of becoming parents. They discussed marriage and they even chose a name for their child. Jack was ecstatic. He loved Erica and looked forward to starting a family with her. Without warning, Erica changed her mind and decided to obtain an abortion. Jack was devastated. He was confused about her change of heart and desperately tried to prevent the abortion. Jack pleaded with Erica but she was determined to end the pregnancy. He also spoke with her father, a priest, and consulted three different attorneys. None of them could help him and he experienced a deep sense of helplessness. As Jack said, "You want to be able to do something, you want to be able to save the baby, and there's nothing you can do."

Jack and Erica's relationship ended a few weeks before

she actually had the abortion. The anger and confusion that Jack felt towards her made it impossible for the relationship to continue. He had lost both his child and the woman he believed would be his wife.

When I met Jack, he said he was still feeling angry and helpless. He also indicated that he was experiencing difficulty concentrating and was unable to sleep at night. During our first meeting, Jack told me that soon after the abortion, he had deliberately become involved in another relationship because he "wanted to forget about what happened." Jack said that it quickly became apparent to him that another relationship "wasn't the answer." He also stated, "the last thing I wanted to do was to hurt somebody else." Jack came to realize that before he could have a healthy and meaningful relationship, he had to work through his anger, helplessness, and grief.

Jack demonstrated a high degree of awareness and acceptance of his feelings. He recognized that his anger and helplessness were responses to his inability to protect his child and to maintain his relationship with Erica. As he said, "a guy is supposed to be able to handle everything." Jack was actually fortunate in that he had close male friends that he could talk to. His friends validated his feelings and this helped Jack to feel that his reaction was "okay."

Because Jack believed that he had done everything he could to prevent the abortion, he was not experiencing a great deal of guilt about the actual abortion. However, Jack was still struggling with a great deal of anger towards Erica and grief over his loss. He also said that he felt troubled by the fact that he could feel such intense anger towards a woman he still loved so much.

I asked Jack if he had thought about forgiving Erica and we talked about the benefits of forgiveness for ourselves as well as for the one who has hurt us. Jack seemed very receptive to considering forgiveness. He knew his negative feelings were justified but also that they were making him miserable. He also continued to have loving feelings toward Erica. Forgiveness seemed, to him, to be a response worth pursuing.

The fact that Jack was able to acknowledge and share his anger enabled him to move right into the forgiveness process. When people will not or cannot acknowledge anger, they may think they have forgiven when actually they have merely traded anger for resentment.

After meeting together for 12 weeks and working towards forgiveness, Jack was able to go to Erica and tell her that he had forgiven her. He also gave her a Christmas gift demonstrating a generous behavioral response. In addition to these positive thoughts and behaviors, Jack evidenced less anger, anxiety, and grief. As Jack began to experience the healing that forgiveness brings, he lovingly offered that healing to Erica.

Through heartache and much hard work, Jack came to understand that forgiveness is not excusing and it does not guarantee a reconciliation with the one who hurt us. He also recognized that forgiveness does not rid us of painful memories. Jack still had difficulty seeing his nieces and nephews as they reminded him of the child he lost. However, he was able to regain a sense of control over his life and to think about his future.

He expressed both caution and hope concerning future relationships: "I'm going to be a hell of a lot more cautious and take things more slowly, but I'm willing to try and I give myself credit for trying." This statement implies that Jack was regaining a sense of self-confidence. It also suggests a focus on the future. Because he was willing to let go of his anger and to forgive Erica, he was no longer trapped in the hurtful past. Instead of focusing on that which was behind him, he was able to envision that which was ahead of him.

Chapter Five

Anger and Forgiveness

THE POST-ABORTION MAN may feel anger, even rage, depending on the circumstances surrounding the abortion. Like Jack, those who were opposed to the abortion and resent their inability to impact the abortion decision are especially vulnerable to intense feelings of anger. This anger may be directed at the partner, the physician, the self and/or others that are believed to have influenced the decision. Sometimes the anger is directed toward a group of people. For example, the anger may be directed at women in general or a specific group of women. Matthew, another one of the men I worked with, told me that he felt rage toward feminists and his anger was triggered every time he heard certain phrases which have now become slogans of the feminist movement: "It's my body," "It's my choice." He was outraged that he had no choice and no voice. He couldn't understand why his partner and our legal system didn't recognize what he believed to be his legitimate rights as an expectant father. Jack, who shared the preceding story, told me that he contacted an attorney in an attempt to prevent his girlfriend from having an abortion. The attorney told him politely and honestly that there was no legal recourse and a woman has complete legal power regarding an abortion decision. Determined to pursue what he believed were his legitimate rights, Jack contacted two more attorneys and was given the same message. There was nothing he or the attorneys could do to prevent his partner from having the abortion. Jack felt that both his girlfriend and our justice system had failed him.

Both Jack and Matthew were in serious relationships with women whom they thought that they could trust. Each of them had seriously discussed marriage with their partners and, upon learning of a pregnancy, had eagerly anticipated marriage and a family. Instead, they found themselves unable to protect their unborn children, confused that the women they loved and trusted could make such a unilateral decision, and deeply saddened that their relationships had ended. Of course they were angry!

Anger is a normal response when we are deeply and unfairly hurt by another. When we have been threatened or injured, we may experience many emotions, but anger is almost always one of those emotions. Most of us are not comfortable with anger. In fact, some people are so uncomfortable with this emotion that they may actually deny their anger and may be completely unaware of their angry feelings.

Even when people recognize that they are angry, they often find the emotion to be unpleasant and difficult to deal with. It is my belief that anger is seldom experienced alone. Rather, people tend to feel both anger and anxiety, to varying degrees, at the same time. Many of us were given a direct or indirect message as children that it wasn't 'nice' to be angry. So, when we feel angry, we also may feel guilty and anxious about our inner hostility. We also may feel anxious because we are aware of the very real danger of expressing our anger in hurtful ways.

Finally, given the fact that anger is often a response to a genuine threat to us, it is understandable that we would feel frightened and anxious as well as angry. When we are threatened and unable to remove the threat, we may feel helpless which can lead to anger. Several of the men who participated in our research observed that their anger was very much a response to their feelings of helplessness. This is a topic which will be further explored in the next chapter.

While most people would not describe anger as a pleasant emotion, it may serve a useful purpose. Sometimes anger is our first clue that we are dealing with a threat or injury. In such a case, examining our anger and its source can help us to better understand our response to the injury and also to begin to explore alternative responses. When channeled into appropriate outlets, anger also can provide the motivation and energy to work toward a worthy goal. For example, various support groups have been started by individuals who experienced a traumatic injury and chose to channel their anger into helping others who experienced similar injuries. Because of the potential energizing effects of anger, some people may even prefer to feel angry rather than depressed.

However, while anger may be useful and energizing, it also can be destructive and exhausting. Intense anger can lead to violent outbursts that hurt ourselves and/or others. Less obvious, but equally destructive, is the long-term, simmering variety of anger that often turns to bitterness and cynicism. This type of anger can be equally damaging. One of our research volunteers said, "My anger was turned inward. I developed a more callous and bitter view of the world." Until he dealt with his anger and expressed it appropriately, he could not get beyond his cynicism. Another man stated, "Anger and getting even are just as destructive as grief. An unforgiving attitude keeps your energy locked in a negative direction that hurts yourself and everyone around you." Such unresolved anger may sabotage not only current relationships with those who have hurt us but also our future relationships. It is no surprise then that the apostle Paul instructed his fellow Christians to "not let the sun go down while you are still angry."[1]

Too often, unresolved anger is displaced unto others who have absolutely no responsibility for the injury that made us angry in the first place. This is referred to as "displacement," the expression of anger (or some other emotion) toward a person other than the one who actually triggered our anger. For example, parents, who were verbally abused during childhood, may find themselves verbally abusing their own children. This unhealthy and destructive expression of anger may continue on in succeeding generations. More will be said about this point in the chapter on relationships.

Another consequence of prolonged and unresolved anger is its effect on our ability to concentrate. One of the men who volunteered for this research told me that he lost his job and had to drop out of school because of his persistent and angry thoughts about his abortion experience. When we continue to replay a hurtful incident in our minds, we may become increasingly angry, unable to concentrate, and physically exhausted. When a powerful emotion like anger is not expressed appropriately or remains unresolved, a tremendous amount of psychological and physical energy may be wasted.

Given the dangers of maintaining an angry state, the obvious solution is to get rid of one's anger. The question, of course, is "How do I do that?" Dr. Richard Fitzgibbons, a psychiatrist, has stated that "When anger develops, there are three mechanisms available for dealing with this emotion. These are denial, expression, and forgiveness."[2] Obviously, if anger is being denied, it can't be dealt with. We also know that destructive expressions of anger hurt both the angry person and the one to whom the expression is directed. That leaves us with the third option, forgiveness.

Dr. Fitzgibbons claims that, "Forgiveness is a powerful therapeutic intervention which frees people from their anger and from the guilt which is often a result of unconscious anger."[3] When people make a conscious decision to forgive, they have decided not to seek revenge or retribution. They have freed themselves as well as their offender. As their anger lessens, so too should their guilt and anxiety. We have seen this to be true in various studies which have utilized a forgiveness intervention with clinical populations.[4,5,6] So, the decision to forgive benefits the injured by decreasing his anger and anxiety and it benefits the offender because the threat of retribution is removed.

The choice to forgive does not mean that one can't express his anger but rather that the means of expression will not entail deliberate damage to the offender. I asked the men who participated in our study to express their anger in a letter written to the person they most blamed for the abortion. The intent was not to actually mail these letters but simply to use them as a safe means of venting anger. While it is not meant to be a 'quick-fix,' this exercise may help the post-abortion man to do the following: 1) more clearly identify who he is really angry at, 2) become more aware of the degree of his anger, and 3) experience some degree of release.

If he finds, after this exercise, that he is actually most angry at himself, then self-forgiveness may be a more immediate issue for him than other-forgiveness. Perhaps he will come to the conclusion that both self-forgiveness and other-forgiveness are issues he would like to work on. That was the experience of the majority of the men that I worked with. The process of forgiving ourselves and the process of forgiving others are not so very different. Self-forgiveness will be discussed in Chapter 7.

If a post-abortion man tries this exercise and finds that his anger is much greater than he would have thought, I would tell him not to be alarmed. Sometimes, an exercise such as this one pushes us to get in touch with feelings we have kept buried. Remember, anger that is denied cannot be resolved while anger that is conscious can be. I warned the men who participated in our research that as we worked through the process of forgiveness, they might experience periods during which they felt worse instead of better. This is not an unusual occurrence. When we deliberately look at a hurtful event and the pain we have suffered, it is not expected to be a pleasant experience. However, we cannot move forward through a healing process if we don't first face reality.

Some men may find that, having written an angry letter, they feel some sense of relief. They expressed their rage on paper, they accept that it is a part of their response to hurt, and they are now wanting to get on with the next step.

If they have not yet made a conscious decision to work toward forgiveness, this may be the time to consider doing so. Both the Christian and the non-Christian may be helped to forgive by reframing his view of the one who hurt him.

The concept of reframing, has been discussed in Chapters 3 and 4. Often, when others hurt us deeply, we see them only in light of the injury they have caused. The injury becomes the frame which we use to view them. If we try to see the larger picture, which might include information about the offenders' perceptions, family, and extenuating circumstances, we can take into consideration these other aspects of the picture and perhaps gain some understanding as to why they behaved as they did.

I asked each of the men I worked with to reframe their views of the women who hurt them by attempting to view these women in a larger context. This context would include what the man knew of her family and her personality. One of the men recalled that his partner was a high achiever. She had grown up in a home where her parents expected a great deal of her and she consistently met their high expectations. Because of her achievements, she became somewhat of the family favorite. It was tacitly assumed that she would always succeed and make her parents proud. When she unexpectedly became pregnant, she did not feel that she could tell her parents as her 'failure' would let them down and violate their beliefs about her. Instead, she chose what seemed to be an easy way out, abortion. I asked this particular man to enlarge his viewing frame even further by including the context of our culture. I pointed out that both he and his partner grew up in a society where abortion was not only legal but was touted by many as solely a woman's right. His partner had, no doubt, repeatedly heard this message and was making a decision that, in her view, seemed reasonable.

As this man came to see his former girlfriend in a larger context, he was able to understand what she did and why she did it. He was also able to feel compassion towards her as he considered the family and societal pressures as she perceived them. This process, of reframing, is critical in helping us to feel empathy and compassion towards the one who hurt us and to continue on in our forgiveness journey. It becomes very difficult to maintain intense anger toward the same person we are coming to feel compassion toward.

Remember, when I speak of reframing and how it can help us to understand and forgive an offender, I am absolutely not talking about excusing the offender. If the one who hurt us had a valid excuse, then there would be nothing to forgive. Reframing is an important tool in helping us to forgive. It is not a means to minimize the offense or to conclude either that the injury was really not so bad or that the one who hurt us couldn't help it. Just so there is no misunderstanding on this point, let me say that I am convinced that some men are deeply and unfairly hurt when their partners choose to obtain an abortion. The anger these men feel is justified because they have been treated unfairly. There is no excuse for the exclusion of fathers when decisions are made about their children's futures. However, if we want to heal and move on after experiencing a devastating injury, then we must be able to develop understanding and compassion towards those who have hurt us.

Not only can reframing help us to forgive a specific person for a specific injury, but it may help us to be more understanding and forgiving in the future. Usually we are able to do something well for one of two reasons. Either we have a natural talent or we have engaged in a good deal of practice. Some people seem to be more empathetic than others. Perhaps they have rather easy-going temperaments and/or have grown up with empathetic parents who were good teachers. Other people seem to have more difficulty seeing the world from another's perspective and might do well to practice reframing.

To help one practice reframing, I would suggest he ask himself some specific questions: First, is it reasonable to pass a global judgment on the one who hurt me based on a single act? Second, does the person who hurt me have some worth simply because she's a fellow human being? Regarding the first question, I would argue that each of us is much too complex to be defined by a single act no matter how hurtful that act may be. Usually, the people most capable of hurting us deeply are those we love the most or, at least, are the people we have a good deal of emotional investment in. We probably wouldn't love these people if we didn't appreciate some good qualities in them. As we remember these qualities, we enlarge the context in which we view and evaluate them. Concerning the second question, I believe that each of us has inherent worth because we are each created by God. If this belief is also a part of your faith or worldview, it may motivate you to see the one who hurt you as having some degree of worth in spite of the offense. Still another question to consider is whether the offender is, in fact, morally inferior to the injured person. The Christian has a clear and absolute answer to this question, "There is no one righteous, not even one."[7] In other words, we have all been pronounced guilty and are in need of forgiveness.

As one practices reframing as a means to develop empathy regarding a specific offense, one may find that he is better able to do so in future hurtful situations. Becoming more proficient at empathizing may foster one's ability to forgive both now and in the future.

Reframing, developing understanding, and empathy do not magically erase all anger. However, as already stated, it is difficult to maintain intense anger and empathy at the same time. As one becomes more empathetic towards his offender, he should also experience a decrease in his anger toward her. In addition, he is more likely to express residual anger in a constructive way.

The injured person may find that it is easier to change his thoughts toward his offender than it is to change his feelings. He may notice that he now has more positive thoughts toward the one who hurt him but that he is still struggling with anger and other negative emotions. This is normal and not uncommon. Although forgiveness is a difficult task, we have found that genuine forgiveness does bring a reduction in negative feelings. The act of reframing in the forgiveness process leads to empathy toward those who have hurt us, which, in turn, enables us to love them. Thus, as the injured follows through on his commitment to forgive, he can expect to experience more positive feelings as well.

Remember too that forgiveness is not forgetting. We have memories that cannot be erased but as the painful emotions diminish, there is room for hope to grow, and where there is hope there is a focus on the future.

Putting the Ideas into Practice

Acknowledge your anger and accept that it is normal to feel angry after being hurt deeply and unfairly. The *feeling* of anger is not immoral but what we *do* with our anger may be immoral.

Use appropriate ways to express your anger such as:

1. Write a letter expressing your anger to the one who hurt you but do not send it.
2. Confront the one who hurt you *if* you can do so with kindness.
3. Talk to God about your anger through prayer.
4. Speak to a trusted parent, friend, or counselor.
5. Physical activity or exercise.

Ask the following questions to facilitate reframing* and to understand why a person behaved as he/she did:

1. What kind of pressures was I/my partner struggling with when I/she made the abortion decision?
2. What were my/her fears? How did these contribute to the abortion decision?
3. How might others (such as friends, family members, or medical personnel) have influenced the decision to choose abortion?
4. Is it fair to condemn someone on the basis of a single act or mistake?
5. Does each and every person have inherent worth simply because they are fellow human beings? If I believe this to be true, then even the one who hurt me has worth as a human being.

The decision to forgive the one who hurt you is a critical turning point. However, full forgiveness takes time and effort; as your thoughts about the one who hurt you become more positive, your feelings toward her will become more positive as well.

*Remember, the purpose of reframing is not to excuse those who have hurt us, but to understand their behavior and to begin to feel compassion for them. As we reframe and come to understand someone's behavior, our thoughts about them may change *before* our feelings change.

Ted's Story

TED WAS IN HIS EARLY twenties when he came to the United States. In a fairly short period of time, he learned the English language and acquired a good job. He also began a relationship with a young woman and they decided to live together. Their relationship lasted for three years and during that time Ted's partner, Michelle, had two abortions.

Ted was opposed to the abortion option each time he learned of Michelle's pregnancy. When I asked Ted why he was opposed to abortion, he told me that there were a number of reasons for his opposition. He did not believe that inconvenience was a justifiable reason to end a pregnancy. Ted also told me that abortion was a violation of his moral beliefs and he stated, "I abhor to kill possibilities." Ted did not view pregnancy as a 'condition' but rather as the beginning of a human life with potential and possibility.

Upon being told of her first pregnancy, Ted stated that

he wanted to continue his relationship with Michelle and offered to support both her and the child. While he tried to dissuade Michelle from having an abortion, he also recognized that the legal choice belonged to her. Although she chose to have an abortion against Ted's wishes, he willingly remained in the relationship. When he was told of her second pregnancy, he again made a genuine offer of support but, once more, Michelle chose to obtain an abortion.

Ted and Michelle's relationship ended within a couple of months following this second abortion. Ted told me that he simply couldn't risk being hurt again. Unfortunately, Ted had already been hurt a great deal. Due to persistent thoughts about the abortions and nagging self-doubts about what he might have said or done to dissuade Michelle, he lost his job. He then went to school but had to drop out because of the persistent, negative thoughts and his inability to concentrate.

When I met Ted, he seemed somewhat depressed and it was obvious that his self-esteem was shaken. He had lost a relationship, a job, and now his hope to further his education. He acknowledged his profound feelings of helplessness and stated "helplessness leads to hopelessness which leads to despair."

While I did not minimize Ted's losses (for they were many), I did point out to him that he had achieved a great deal. I sincerely could not imagine accomplishing what he had in such a short period of time. I also observed that, in spite of his personal pain, he was actively involved in a local volunteer program. My goal was to help Ted to see himself in a larger context. Although he was truly helpless in terms of preventing Michelle's abortions, he was not a helpless person. He had learned a new language, acclimated himself to a foreign culture, was helping another through volunteer work, and he had taken the initiative to seek help for his post-abortion pain; these facts demonstrated that he was not completely helpless.

As Ted came to see himself in a more realistic way, his feelings of helplessness decreased and his hope increased. He was able to alter his expectations of himself and his future.

Eventually, Ted was able to forgive Michelle and to stop condemning himself for something he legally couldn't prevent. He now has a new job that he enjoys and is competent at. His passion for life is apparent and he is hopeful that he will find a woman with whom he can have a meaningful and trusting relationship.

Chapter Six

HELPLESSNESS AND FORGIVENESS

AS STATED PREVIOUSLY, Chapters 5 through 9 cover certain problem areas in the same order they were covered in the research intervention. The decision to put anger before helplessness was deliberate. We believed that it would be easier for men to acknowledge and discuss their feelings of anger than their feelings of helplessness. Most people don't like to feel helpless and out of control. Although the gender role expectations of our culture have changed considerably in the last twenty years, men are still under enormous pressure to contain their emotions and take charge. Therefore, it seemed sensible to begin with what may be perceived as a more acceptable emotion (anger) and then to discuss what might be more threatening (helplessness).

Feelings of helplessness are frequently reported by men who have been hurt by an abortion experience. Like anger, helplessness is a normal and valid response to an injury, particularly the injury inflicted by abortion. Our society, our legal system, and female biology do, in fact, render men somewhat helpless regarding abortion. Much of our society continues to espouse abortion as a woman's right and the fetus as the woman's property. The man is not even viewed as co-owner. Legally, all power is granted to a woman regarding an abortion decision. This is true even if the woman is married. Finally, there is the biological fact that while both male and female contributions are required to produce a child, only the female can carry that child for the first nine months of its life. It is not surprising then that a man who opposes his partner's decision to abort their child would feel helpless.

In addition to the societal, legal, and biological constraints men face, they also are denied the expression of what I believe is a basic instinct. Most people have heard the expression, "maternal instinct." I would argue that there is an equally powerful "paternal instinct" which motivates men to protect and care for their families. When a man finds out he is to become a father and his partner deliberately ends the pregnancy, his paternal instinct is violated. He may feel helpless because of his inability to act on that instinct. As one of the men involved in our research said, "You want to be able to do something. You want to be able to save the baby and there's nothing you can do!" Another said, "I really felt for that baby. I did everything I could but it was her reasons that she listened to when she decided to have the abortion. There was not a damn thing I could do. She told me over and over, 'This is not your body.'"

As noted in Chapter 5, helplessness may contribute to anger. One of the research participants stated, "When I think about the abortion, I feel enormously helpless. The helplessness sometimes brings tears to my eyes, angry tears." Another man told me "I was powerless, that made me angry... and the fact that I wanted to be a father and this woman just took that away from me."

The men who were opposed to abortion from the time they learned of the pregnancy were very much aware of their feelings of helplessness. Some of the other men described themselves as experiencing a general sense of confusion when they first learned that their partners were pregnant and that this confusion caused them to feel helpless. They were confused about the role they were expected to play. They knew that their female partners had the power to make a unilateral abortion decision so they tended to see their role as one of support. They assumed that they should support whatever decision she made and sincerely attempted to do so. It was later, after the actual abortions occurred, that they became aware of feeling both helpless and angry.

It is not unusual, during a crisis situation such as an unplanned pregnancy, for people to feel out of control and confused. A crisis usually requires action but how do we choose an appropriate course of action when we're also feeling confused? Whatever course of action we choose brings consequences. Those consequences and their ramifications are what we have to live with. The men in this study, whether they chose to argue against the abortion or to initially support their partners' abortion decisions, experienced painful consequences. Helplessness was just one of those consequences.

Like anger, helplessness regarding one situation may manifest itself in others. A man may feel a generalized sense of helplessness or he may be able to identify certain areas in which he feels helpless. As Ted said, helplessness leads to hopelessness and hopelessness to despair. He was trying to describe a general feeling of helplessness that had permeated his attitude toward all of life. Recall that Ted had come to the United States without even knowing English. In only a few years, he had learned the English language and acquired a very good job. As he put it, "I was working for the American dream, but now I think, 'Why? For what?'" For Ted, helplessness had affected his whole outlook on life. Another post-abortion man told me that while his sense of helplessness had not affected his general outlook, it had definitely caused him to fear relationships. Without a guarantee that he would have at least equal power in a relationship, the risks inherent in any relationship were simply not worth taking.

Both helplessness and anger are often responses to what we perceive as a violation of justice. We live with legal rules, cultural rules, family rules, and our own personal code. These all contribute to our individual sense of justice. When our beliefs about justice are violated, we may need to alter our worldview or, at least, to recognize that everybody doesn't play by the same rules.

I told all of the men involved in this research that I did not perceive them as totally helpless because if that were true, then they would not have taken the initiative to contact me. They would not have continued to meet with me for 12 weeks and they would not have completed the study. A post-abortion man who is reading this book in an attempt to heal, is also not completely helpless. He has taken a step forward and, I presume, is trying to focus on his future rather than his past. He is taking a risk by facing his pain and that is, by no means, a helpless thing to do.

An exercise which may help a man to decrease his sense of helplessness, is to list the ways by which he might help another man who has experienced an abortion. I found it to be very interesting that our research participants consistently identified simply 'listening' to other men as helpful. Active listening is therapeutic for a number of reasons. First, it gives the speaker the message that he and his words are of interest to us. Second, it helps us to stay on track and really hear what is being said. If we are preoccupied with what we're going to say next, then we aren't really giving the speaker our undivided attention. Finally, if we can listen objectively and with acceptance, the speaker and his experience are validated. This, I believe, is of critical importance because much of society does not attend to, much less validate, the post-abortion man's experience. He is, at best, ignored in the abortion debate and, at worst, told he is not worthy to participate.

An abortion decision is a permanent one. It can't be undone and those involved will be permanently altered by its effects. All of life's experiences, both the good and the bad, change us. Like the men who participated in this research, other post-abortion men can choose to learn from their experience and to perhaps use that experience to help others. One way we can extract something good out of a very bad situation is to try and learn from it. The knowledge we gain can help us to avoid pain in the future and to help others. As we do this, we lose our feeling of helplessness and regain a sense of both competence and usefulness.

The choice to forgive can also help to rid us of helplessness. The fact that forgiveness is, first of all, a choice means that it is an act of will. Forgiveness is not a passive acceptance of what has happened to us. Rather, it is an active response to what has happened to us. Taking deliberate action helps us to feel in control of life again or at least in control of ourselves. When we don't forgive, we are surrendering control to the one who hurt us. That adds to our sense of helplessness. Colleen Benson, a psychologist, contends that "one of the most serious consequences of lacking forgiveness is that we become bonded to those we need to forgive."[1] When we choose to forgive, however, we free ourselves as well as others.

While genuine forgiveness fosters a sense of control over the self, pseudoforgiveness seeks to control others. This may occur when an individual claims to forgive but is actually attempting to manipulate the offender by making her feel morally inferior. For example, if an injured person claims to have forgiven his offender but then repeatedly reminds her of the offense and of his generous response, he is manipulating and not forgiving. He is practicing a form of pseudoforgiveness.

Genuine forgiveness is an act of strength and not of weakness. In order to truly forgive another, we must choose to bear the pain caused by the injury. In other words, we must consciously and willfully choose to avoid transmitting our pain to others. There are a number of ways that a man might transmit his pain to another including abuse or neglect. A more subtle way, however, is through emotional distancing. For example, a post-abortion man who is hurting may avoid any form of intimate communication with his partner. She may ask him about his lack of communication and he may be confused and unaware that he has been withdrawn. This may be his first clue that his attempt to protect himself has been painful to another.

Actually, his pain may be lessened and therefore easier to carry if he shares it with another. Some may choose to speak to a friend or counselor and others may choose to give their pain to God through prayer. The decision to forgive and bear one's pain is a choice that entails both courage and compassion for others. It requires strength of mind and heart. For this reason, genuine forgiveness is incompatible with helplessness. To those who feel that they are helpless even to forgive, I would suggest that they seek counseling from one who values forgiveness. Those who believe in God may also seek God's help as they attempt to do that which He requires.

In sum, helplessness is a normal reaction among post-abortion men. It is a logical response to the barriers men face when dealing with abortion. However, the helplessness the post-abortion man may be feeling is not total or permanent. I told the men I worked with that their attempt to find healing was proof of this. If they had been completely helpless, they would not have contacted me and become involved in the intervention program. When they made the decision to forgive, they reached a turning point. They no longer needed to feel helpless and under the control of those who hurt them. Instead, they took back control of their own lives and they did so in an honorable and loving way.

The man who has been hurt by abortion may find that his experience has enabled him to relate to other post-abortion men in a powerful way. He may discover that he is now in a position to be *helpful* rather than helpless. After all, who could provide other post-abortion men with more genuine understanding and support than one who has actually experienced the same loss?

Putting the Ideas into Practice

Acknowledge your feeling of helplessness and accept that it is a normal response when one is confronted with a crisis situation. Remember, feeling helpless in *one* situation does not mean that you will be helpless in *all* situations.

To decrease feelings of helplessness:

1. Talk about your sense of helplessness with someone you trust, someone who will listen and be supportive of you.
2. Make a list of the ways you could help other men or women who are either facing an unexpected pregnancy or who have experienced abortion. Such a list could include how you might help an individual to avoid a crisis pregnancy, how you might counsel one who is facing a crisis pregnancy, and/or how you might help him/her after an abortion.
3. Take your newfound knowledge and *apply* it by sharing your story, volunteering at your local crisis pregnancy center, and/or by being sensitive and available to other post-abortion men and women.
4. Make a list of your talents, abilities, and/or accomplishments.

To find meaning in your suffering:

1. List all of the things that you have learned from your experience. These may be lessons about yourself, about others, or about God.
2. Share what you have learned with others who may be hurting. In this way, you may help them to find meaning too.

Forgiveness is a difficult task, be patient with yourself as you work toward forgiving the one who hurt you.

Bill's Story

"SHE WAS THE FIRST GIRL that I ever dated steady. I was 22 and she was 20. I am 46 now. We went out for about two and a half years. I hadn't been out much with girls and she was the first girl that I had sex with. It was something new and wonderful to me. I know that she loved me and she told me that.

"I'll never forget when we walked from the doctor's office to the car and how she cried (after learning of the pregnancy). I felt really sorry for her. I was just kind of in shock for a few minutes.... I really never believed it would happen to us. She decided a little while after she stopped crying that she wanted an abortion. I offered to marry her although I was not very positive about it. From the doctor's office, we went to see the priest. We told the priest about the situation and also that she wanted an abortion. I will never forget his words, 'It's her decision – you have nothing to say about it – she has to live with that decision, not you.' So after he spoke to us, I decided that it was her decision and a couple of days later, we went for the abortion.

"It was a sad day in my life. I hated that abortion clinic and I felt sorry for her after it was over. It looked like all of the life had been taken out of her. She was also very sick on the way home. I will never forget the look on her face and as long as I live, I will never forget that day.

"Our relationship ended about a month after the abortion. I just didn't want to touch her or anything else and we grew farther and farther apart. Things were never the same after the abortion.

"I wish every day of my life that it would not have happened. Only I know how sorry I am in my heart, and if there was any way I could change it, I would, even if it meant giving up my life. I guess it's the loss you feel... I think it's something you never get over. I think it's made me realize how precious life is.

"I feel I have pretty much resolved my negative feelings regarding the abortion. I think about it a lot. I also pray about it. I know in my heart and God knows how sorry I am. I think I've learned a lot from that mistake. I'm trying to do good things in my life and I work at a crisis pregnancy center. I don't think I'd be doing that if the abortion hadn't happened.

"I think the hardest thing to do is to forgive yourself. I think right now I'm pretty much there. I know that God is a loving and forgiving God and He is very merciful. I think that one of the most important things for post-abortive people to do is to go to God, let Him know you're sorry, and ask for forgiveness... and go to your child and ask for forgiveness.

"I'm still a little scared of relationships and of getting intimate with someone. I know that I don't ever want to get myself in an unplanned pregnancy situation again. That's the most frightening thing to me. I think that it's really sad that men have no rights to protect their children from abortion. I know for me it was just such a helpless feeling. Men are just as much victims of abortion as women... yet we have nothing to say. I hope maybe that someday that will change.

"I would love to be a father someday. I think children are the greatest gifts that we can be given in life. Abortion has made the value of life seem so small."

Chapter Seven

GUILT AND FORGIVENESS

THE MAJORITY OF THE MEN who participated in our research said that they were experiencing difficulty in forgiving themselves. Like Bill, they found self-forgiveness to be a difficult task.

Often, when we are feeling guilty for having committed a wrong, we also feel ashamed. When we blame ourselves for a hurtful act, we may feel guilty. When we actually experience or expect to experience condemnation from others, we may feel shame. Both of these emotions are normal responses when we do something that violates our conscience, faith, and/or worldview. Like anger, these emotions can serve a healthy purpose. They are the signals that tell us it is time to make amends or change course. On the other hand, unresolved guilt and shame can eat away at us and create prolonged anxiety which makes it very difficult to enjoy life.

The post-abortion man who finds that he is often thinking about his offense and condemning himself for his behavior is probably using up a good deal of psychological energy. This can be just as exhausting as the expenditure of physical energy. Constant thoughts about his failure also may interfere with his ability to focus or to relate to others.

He also may find himself comparing his situation with that of the person he injured. He may believe that the one he harmed is worse off than himself and that the damage he inflicted is permanent. If he hurt both himself and another, he may believe that he has permanently damaged himself as well. All of these thoughts may be adding to the weight of his guilt and remorse. His sense of self, that is, his beliefs about who he is and what kind of person he is may be quite shaken. Perhaps his experience has brought him some new insights about himself and he is seeing himself in a new, more accurate light, or perhaps he is condemning himself as completely worthless.

As the post-abortion man becomes more aware of both the nature and frequency of his thoughts, he will, hopefully, be motivated to consider self-forgiveness as a healing option. Self-forgiveness, like forgiving another, can rid us of negative emotions (or at least decrease their intensity) and pave the way for more effective, more joyful living.

Just as reframing can help us to forgive another, it can help us to forgive ourselves. If we recall all of the factors that may have contributed to the act which we now condemn, we may come to understand why we behaved as we did. Understanding our behavior doesn't excuse us, of course, but understanding may enable us to eventually feel compassion toward ourselves and to forgive ourselves.

Some people may claim that self-forgiveness is a dangerous endeavor. They may believe that self-forgiveness is nothing more than a rationalization for bad behavior. Others may reason that self-forgiveness is impossible due to an inability to be objective about one's own behavior. There are Christians who would argue that self-forgiveness is, at best, a moot point in light of divine forgiveness. According to such an argument, one who has received forgiveness from God has no need to subsequently forgive himself. Other Christians may view self-forgiveness, at worst, as a usurpation of God's authority. C.S. Lewis suggested still another Christian view of self-forgiveness when he said, "I think that if God forgives us we must forgive ourselves. Otherwise it is almost like setting up ourselves as a higher tribunal than Him."[1] I would argue that when we accept God's forgiveness but do not forgive ourselves, we cause God to grieve and prevent our full healing.

Nevertheless, I have spoken with numerous post-abortion men and women who have clearly stated that even though they felt confident God had forgiven them, they still struggled with self-condemnation. They specifically identified "self-forgiveness" as a problem they had to deal with.

Perhaps the disagreements concerning self-forgiveness are due to confusion regarding the definition of this concept. Self-forgiveness may be defined as the cessation of self-punishment and self-condemnation and the merciful acceptance of the self as a valuable human being in spite of one's vulnerability to sin or hurtful acts. Healthy self-forgiveness requires that two conditions be met. First, the individual must recognize his moral wrong. Second, if the wrong has resulted in harm to another, he demonstrates a desire to receive forgiveness from the one he has injured.

I asked the men I worked with to identify exactly what it was that they felt guilty about. Was it the relationship, the pregnancy, or the abortion? For some, it was more than one of these. This question helped them to identify both the wrong(s) they had committed and the person(s) whom they had hurt.

One of the research participants told me that he felt guilty about his relationship with his former partner. He felt that he should have known better than to get involved with a woman who, although an adult, was considerably younger than he was. Regarding the actual abortion, however, he stated that, "What has helped me with the guilt is knowing that I've done everything I could, whether it was trying to stay with her, trying to support her, trying to forgive her." This man was able to clearly separate his responsibility from his partner's. Another one of the men said, "I feel guilty about the pregnancy but not the abortion because I didn't have any say in it. I didn't even know [about the abortion] until weeks later." This man was also clear about his responsibility. Being able to identify exactly what they were and were not guilty of helped these men to work towards self-forgiveness.

Another participant was initially confused about responsibility. He found himself asking, "Was it me? Did I do anything to cause this?" Although he was adamantly opposed to both of his partner's abortions, he still felt a vague sense of guilt and self-doubt. He found himself preoccupied with these questions to the point where he was having difficulty concentrating on anything else. As we examined his actual behavior within the relationship, it became clear that he was taking on more responsibility than was justified. Both times his partner discovered that she was pregnant, he had offered to support her and the child. In fact, their relationship continued after the first abortion. Following the second abortion, this man decided that he no longer wanted to risk being hurt again and the relationship ended. He came to recognize that while he bore some responsibility for conception, he was not responsible for the abortions. He was then able to distinguish between justifiable guilt and unhealthy self-doubt.

Still other men, like Bill, felt guilty about being in sexual relationships with women they weren't married to. These men also felt guilty about the pregnancies that resulted from these relationships. While they acknowledged that self-forgiveness was an issue for them, they recognized their more immediate need was to repent and receive forgiveness from God. For some of these men, the assurance of God's forgiveness seemed to eliminate the self-forgiveness issue. Others, who were certain that God had forgiven them, still found it difficult to forgive themselves.

One of the men in our study felt guilty for actively supporting his partner's abortion. Having been abandoned by his own father, he felt that he had proven himself to be a failure as a parent just as his own father was. This man was able to make significant progress toward forgiving himself. However, he stated that he could only move so far in the self-forgiveness process because, as an agnostic, he didn't believe in a "higher power." He recognized the limitations of self-forgiveness. That is, he realized that he needed to receive forgiveness from another, outside himself, in order to fully experience the release that comes with self-forgiveness. Nonetheless, even as a non-believer, he was able to make progress in his self-forgiveness journey. He was able to do this by admitting his guilt, coming to understand his behavior, and recognizing that he was still a worthy human being. He also found it helpful to share his experience with his mother and be reassured of her love and acceptance toward him.

Before the post-abortion man can begin to work toward self-forgiveness, it is critical that he determine: 1) if he is confusing guilt with either regret or self-doubt; 2) what it is that he feels guilty about and whether his guilt is justified; and 3) whom he has injured, himself and/or another. While most of the men in our study said they felt guilty, all of them struggled with regret and self-doubt. It is natural, and often healthy, for us to take stock of ourselves following a loss, particularly the loss of a relationship. When we acknowledge responsibility, we may gain new insights about ourselves that will enable us to be kinder and wiser in the future. However, if our self-esteem is severely shaken by the loss, we may assume responsibility for something that was, in reality, out of our control. A man who sincerely attempts to support his partner and unborn child cannot be held accountable for her decision to abort. If he were to tell me that he felt guilty for the abortion, I would suggest that he is actually feeling regret or self-doubt.

The post-abortion man may have difficulty identifying the specific cause of his guilt because it is difficult for him to separate the pregnancy from the abortion. He may know with a certainty that he could not prevent the abortion yet reason that if he had not impregnated his partner, then his child would not have died. While there is surely some logic to this reasoning, it confuses justified and groundless guilt.

Let's assume a particular man is careless with birth control. His partner becomes pregnant. He is justifiably guilty for causing a pregnancy. He loves his partner and makes a genuine offer to support her and the child. She argues for abortion. He then pleads with her to reconsider and restates his offer of support. Nonetheless, she decides to obtain an abortion. This is her legal right. The man has no other recourse to alter her decision. Thus, he is not justifiably guilty for the abortion.

Suppose another man is quite careful in the use of birth control. In spite of his care, his partner becomes pregnant.

She states that she wants to have an abortion. He feels confused and assumes that he should support her decision. Later, perhaps months or even years later, he becomes aware of a heavy burden of guilt. In this case, the man may be experiencing justifiable guilt for passively supporting the abortion of his child. He also may experience justifiable guilt for violating his own code of ethics or God's laws. His guilt may be due to the injury to his child, to himself, and to his God.

Still another example would be the Christian man who experiences guilt about a sexual relationship outside of marriage that leads to pregnancy. This man is experiencing justifiable guilt because he has violated the teachings of his faith. He needs to seek and receive forgiveness from God before he can forgive himself.

An exercise which may help the post-abortion man to become more clear concerning his guilt is to write a letter asking for forgiveness. First, he will need to determine who he would write such a letter to. It may be written to his partner, his unborn child, or perhaps to God. One of our research volunteers decided to address his letter to himself. Often, when we hurt another, we feel guilty not only for the pain we caused the other person, but also because we have failed to live up to our own standards or code based upon our religious beliefs. In such a case, we may need to both receive forgiveness from another and to forgive ourselves. While self-forgiveness is the focus of this chapter, I do not want to minimize the importance of seeking forgiveness from those we have wronged. In fact, I would encourage a man to go to those he has offended and ask for their forgiveness, whether it be from another person or from God. There is, of course, the very real possibility that he will not receive the forgiveness he seeks from another person. If that person is his former partner, she may not yet be ready to offer forgiveness to him. On the other hand, he can rest assured that God will forgive him and also help him to be patient with those who are not yet able to do so. In terms of self-forgiveness, a man may find it helpful to speak with a friend, parent, or pastor. Confession can be a powerful means of alleviating guilt.

As the man deliberately analyzes his guilt and its source(s), he may find that some of his guilt is valid while some is not. Perhaps he has been too hard on himself concerning events that were not in his control. This exercise is not expected to rid him of all guilt but it may help to express and clarify his guilt.

After he becomes aware of what has caused him to feel guilty, he can begin to work toward its resolution. The resolution of guilt is healthy because unresolved guilt can lead to depression, anger toward the self, and even self-punishing behaviors. In addition, guilt, like anger, tends to be accompanied by anxiety, another unpleasant emotion.

As the post-abortion man comes to the conclusion that he needs to resolve his guilt, he may at least consider self-forgiveness as an option. Hopefully, he will then decide to actively work towards self-forgiveness. While a commitment to forgive another or the self is a critical step in the forgiveness process, it is by no means the end of or the equivalent of forgiveness. There is still a good deal of work to be done including reframing.

The post-abortion man may need to reframe his picture of himself. An unplanned pregnancy is a crisis situation. Confusion is a normal response to a crisis and unfortunately may lead to regrettable choices. A man who has experienced an abortion may have had no previous experience dealing with such a situation. That fact alone could have influenced his behavior. If he feels compelled to judge himself harshly, he might try to take into account his inexperience, his fear, and his anxiety. Once again, I want to stress, that the singular purpose of reframing is to develop empathy and compassion. I am not suggesting one excuse himself if he is justifiably guilty of some offense such as encouraging an abortion or abandoning his partner. I am suggesting, however, that he view himself in as large a context as possible, a larger context than that of the relationship or the abortion. A single act does not define who he is as a person. Even if he finds it difficult to enumerate his good qualities, he may consider that he has inherent worth as a human being, a creation of God. When we consider ourselves as members of the human race, we are seeing ourselves in the largest of contexts. If the man believes that every individual human has inherent worth, then it is only logical that he apply that belief to himself.

As he recalls his individual situation and identifies all of the pressures he faced, he may become aware of his own suffering due to the consequences of his actions. Recognition of his suffering may, in turn, enable him to feel compassion toward himself. When he can begin to feel compassion for himself, even while he condemns his behavior, he has made considerable progress in the self-forgiveness journey.

The next critical step is "absorbing the pain." This step is identical to the corresponding step in the process of forgiving another. Whether one's pain is due to the act of another or of the self, it can be transmitted to others. Unless we make a deliberate effort to control destructive expressions of our pain, we may inadvertently pass that pain and suffering unto innocent others. This can result in damaged relationships and endless cycles of hurt. Also, making a deliberate effort to master one's pain serves to prevent even more guilt for the one who is working toward self-forgiveness. While the post-abortion man should be encouraged to share his pain with an empathetic listener, he should also try to become aware of how he may be communicating his pain to others in destructive ways and to make a conscious effort to avoid doing so.

As progress is made toward self-forgiveness, the individual experiences more of the benefits of self-forgiveness including finding meaning in the suffering and perhaps even a new purpose in life. Finding meaning in one's suffering may be accomplished by asking, "What have I learned from this?" or "What possible good has come out of my suffering?" The ability to extract something good or useful out of a bad situation enables us to put the past into a larger perspective and to take something valuable into the future. The individual also may recognize that, in the past, he has both offered forgiveness to others and received forgiveness from them. This recognition may strengthen his resolve to forgive himself. This identification with others also may remind the individual of the universality of his experience. The knowledge that he is not alone normalizes his experience and may allow him to seek support from others.

The man who has been hurt by abortion also may find a new purpose in life that is directly related to his experience. For example, some men I know have chosen to counsel other post-abortion men. Who, better than they, could truly understand such an experience? Several others have become more vocal about their pro-life views. They are hoping to affect legislation. All of the men in our study expressed an increased awareness of and sensitivity toward other post-abortion men. Their ability to empathize has developed out of their shared experiences. Finally, many of the men said that they found themselves thinking about forgiveness in general and in relation to other hurts that they had experienced. Perhaps, for these men, forgiveness will become an essential part of their perceived purpose in life.

As one reaches the point of self-forgiveness, one experiences freedom from the burden of guilt. For the post-abortion man, there may always be regret and remorse, but self-forgiveness brings a lightening of the emotional pain and the ability to move on.

For the man who continues to be troubled by thoughts of self-condemnation, I would suggest he reread the story of the prodigal son in the gospel of Luke (chapter 15:11-24).[2] Verse 20 of this chapter is especially powerful. In this verse, we read about the wayward son's decision to go home and his father's response to his homecoming; "So he, [the prodigal son], got up and went to his father. But while he was still a long way off, his father saw him and was filled with compassion for him; he ran to his son, threw his arms around him and kissed him." We see here a beautiful picture of God's response to us when we choose to approach Him. Notice that God's response was at the moment He saw His son even though the son was still a "long way off." God approaches us too at the very moment we turn back to Him. He doesn't wait for us to make the journey alone, but rather, He literally runs to meet us and accompany us back to where we belong.

If the post-abortion man can receive God's forgiveness and also forgive himself, he can experience psychological healing and perhaps foster the healing of others as well.

Putting the Ideas into Practice

Acknowledge your guilt and accept that it is normal and healthy to feel guilty when we have failed morally or hurt another. Guilt may serve a healthy purpose by letting us know that we have committed an offense and that we need to do what we can to make amends.

Try to determine exactly what you are truly responsible for. You may be responsible for causing a pregnancy but not for an abortion decision particularly if you tried to talk your partner out of the decision. On the other hand, you may be responsible for the abortion if you abandoned your partner or passively left the decision to her.

Confess your guilt to a person you trust. This person could be a friend, parent, clergyperson, or counselor. It is important to choose someone who believes that your pain is real.

Write a letter to the one(s) from whom you are seeking forgiveness. This may be to your partner, your child, or to God.

Whenever possible, go to those you have hurt and ask for their forgiveness. You can rest assured that God will forgive you and that He will help you to be patient with those who may not yet be ready to forgive you.

To facilitate self-forgiveness, reframe* your failure by asking yourself the following questions:

1. What kinds of pressure was I under when the decision to abort was made? Was I overwhelmed with feelings such as fear and confusion?
2. Do I believe that every person has inherent worth as a human being? If my answer is "yes," then am I not a worthy human as well?

3. Is it fair to condemn myself based on a single moral failure no matter how great that failure may have been?

Self-forgiveness can be just as difficult as forgiving another. Be patient with yourself.

*Remember, the purpose of reframing is not to excuse ourselves but to better understand why we behaved as we did. As we reframe and come to understand our behavior, we may still condemn our behavior but we will begin to feel compassion for ourselves as vulnerable human beings.

Cal's Story

CAL IS A YOUNG MAN in his early twenties. He was living with his girlfriend, Barb, when she became pregnant. He wanted to marry her and raise the child. Initially, Barb agreed but shortly after, she decided to have an abortion. Cal said that he tried to convince her otherwise but she was adamant. Cal recalls she kept referring to "her body, her choice, and her child." He was confused that she didn't recognize his legitimate interest in the outcome of the pregnancy. Barb even threatened to tell others that Cal forced her to have the abortion if he talked to anyone about it. Cal then told her that he refused to pay for "killing my child" and would not accompany her to the abortion clinic. Following the abortion, the relationship ended but Cal continued to pay Barb's rent and support a child she had previously while married to another man. After several months, Cal terminated the financial aid.

At our first meeting, Cal expressed a great deal of

ambivalence toward Barb. He said he still loved her but was also very angry with her. He also said that he felt foolish to have continued to give her money for so long after the relationship ended. In his words, "She really took me for a ride, but I still care a lot for her."

Cal was aware of his mental rehearsal of the abortion experience. In fact, he stated that he thought about it "all the time." He was also aware of the difficulty he had trusting women since Barb had lied to him and failed to respond to what he believed to be a more than just offer. Cal told me that he used to trust people until they proved him wrong and said, "but now I don't trust anybody until they prove themselves." After discussing forgiveness and emphasizing that it is not the same thing as acceptance or excusing, Cal stated that he was willing to work toward forgiveness.

As we discussed his partner's characteristics and life history, he was able to understand her possible thoughts and motivations. As he said, "If I put myself in her shoes, I can see why she made that choice." Cal wasn't excusing Barb's decision to go ahead with the abortion against his wishes, but he was attempting to understand that decision and to feel compassion towards her. He recalled that her husband had deserted her and their child, and he recognized that she may have been unable to trust Cal as a result.

Although Cal verbalized that he was "glad to be involved" in our research, he said that he wished he could get an explanation from Barb. I encouraged him to contact her, but warned him that he might not get the answers he was looking for.

Following his contact with Barb, Cal told me that he felt the meeting was very valuable because "it just clicked." He was referring to an internal release of the nagging and negative emotions he had carried for so many months. Cal still had not gotten a satisfactory explanation from Barb but he had at least regained a sense of control and of assurance concerning his own perception of their relationship. At this point, Cal was able to speak of Barb with genuine compassion and understanding. While he was still very much aware of the loss he had suffered and would always grieve, he was also more optimistic and hopeful concerning the future than he had been previously.

Near the end of our time together, Cal became involved with a woman that he was very excited about. This was positive news since he had said that he really wasn't interested in relationships when I first met him. In fact, he told me that the few times he did go out with a woman, he would "tell her right up front" all about his abortion experience in order to make sure that she understood that he would "never go through that again." The fact that he was willing to risk being hurt again says much about his renewed faith in himself.

Chapter Eight

Relationship Problems and Forgiveness

BOTH MEN AND WOMEN may experience relationship problems following an abortion. Depending upon the source cited, anywhere from 25% to 70% of relationships end within a few months after the abortion occurs.[1,2] All of our post-abortion research participants experienced the end of their relationships with their partners.

Whenever a relationship fails, the people involved may feel frightened about future relationships. In the case of a relationship that included physical intimacy, that fear may be even more pronounced. The post-abortion man may believe that his partner's choice to abort was a rejection of himself as well as of his child. He may feel that he has failed in his ability to maintain a relationship and question his ability to do so in the future. He may question his ability to protect others. He also may believe that others can't be trusted to behave fairly in relationships.

The following comments were made by the men who

participated in our research:

> "It's very difficult to get into a relationship and very difficult to get out of a relationship... it's very hurtful... you cannot design yourself not to hurt or not to want or not to miss a person... if that is going to happen, why bother?"

> "Now if I meet a person [a woman], instead of being enthusiastic about a relationship, I think about how it will end up being another stack of baggage for me to handle."

> "It's harder for me to talk to people and trust them, especially females."

> "I don't want to get close emotionally, I'm just so skeptical of relationships."

> "I thought, now I can never be with a woman again because of the risk, because of the anger, because I don't need this headache. This could happen again."

> "If you continue to be in a relationship with someone [after an abortion], it's going to change, no question about it. In my case, it was the principle cause of our divorce. It was a loss that was never dealt with."

> "I lost a lot of my confidence, my self-esteem. I'm not going to let my heart go as quickly anymore."

It is apparent that each of these men was anxious and hesitant about future relationships. All of them stated that they never, ever wanted to experience another abortion. Some of the men had absolutely no interest in pursuing a new relationship. Others were somewhat open to the possibility of another relationship but only under specific conditions. Whether they were somewhat open or totally opposed to getting involved with another woman, all of the men had the same concern, that of self-protection. It is only natural for us to want to avoid pain and to protect ourselves. If a relationship ends because our view of justice is violated, we may become especially fearful of trusting another.

Just as anger and guilt can serve a useful purpose, so too can fear. Fear that is rational, that is, fear that is based on a real threat is a survival signal. It motivates us to avoid that which may be a danger to us. Only when our fear controls us does it become a problem.

It may be helpful for the post-abortion man to think of his fear as temporary and as providing him with a much needed 'time out.' When a relationship ends, we usually need a period of time in which to heal. We need time to reevaluate the lost relationship and our role in that relationship. When an individual doesn't allow for a healing period and jumps right into another relationship, the process of healing may be short-circuited. For example, a man may enter into a new relationship too quickly in order to avoid facing his fears and/or to avoid loneliness. He also may end up being drawn to a similar woman or a similar relationship as he attempts to reenact the conflict he hasn't yet dealt with. This reconstruction of his previous relationship may represent his unconscious effort to undo the mistakes he made in that prior relationship.

It may be useful for the man to monitor his thoughts about the lost relationship in terms of both content and frequency. This may help him to identify the focus of his fear and to determine how realistic his fear is. He may find himself thinking that women in general can't be trusted or that he'll never be able to have a meaningful relationship with another woman. If so, he might consider the fact that one woman really doesn't represent the entire female population.

The odds are actually quite high that some women share his goals and values. We are, after all, people before we are either male or female. If he finds that he is fearful of ever having a successful relationship, I would remind him that our feelings can and do change. While he may be frightened now, he may feel considerably more confident and optimistic in the future. As the individual monitors his thoughts, he becomes more aware of them and begins to recognize the effects of those thoughts on his feelings and behavior. Furthermore, as he attempts to substitute his current thoughts with more realistic ones, he replaces unhealthy thoughts with healthy ones. The intent of monitoring one's thinking is not to discount valid fear but rather to acquire some control over it.

Another exercise which may help him to reestablish hope concerning future relationships is to make a list of the qualities or characteristics he would use to describe the ideal relationship. Of course, ideal or perfect relationships don't exist in reality but, as he reviews his list, he may realize that many of the qualities are attainable most of the time. While all relationships have their ups and downs, they can still be based on fairly stable characteristics of the individuals involved and on rather predictable patterns of interaction between them. For example, most of our research participants listed humor and friendship when doing this exercise. It's reasonable to expect that a partner with a good sense of humor will demonstrate her humor most of the time. It is also realistic to expect that people who describe themselves as "friends" will behave in a friendly manner to each other most of the time. However, none of us is on our best behavior all of the time. In any relationship, the people involved will, at times, let each other down. The risk of being hurt or hurting another is inherent in any relationship.

That's reality. However, we don't have to expect all relationships to be the same.

Just as individuals have unique personalities and characteristics, so too do relationships. Each person in the relationship brings his/her own individual attributes and ways of relating to others. Also, each of our relationships changes us in some way for good or bad. So, with every new relationship we enter, we come as a somewhat different person because of all of our previous experiences. How we process or deal with past relationships will affect who we are in future relationships. If we have experienced a deep and unjust hurt in a past relationship, I believe that choosing to forgive the one who hurt us will greatly increase our chances of having healthy future relationships. This is because genuine forgiveness releases us from the past and from the control of those who have hurt us.

Two steps or variables of the process model in Table 1 are of particular importance when discussing forgiveness and relationships. These are step 8, "insight into a possibly altered just world view," and step 15, "acceptance and absorption of the pain." Each of these concepts has been discussed previously but will be reviewed in the context of relationships.

When we are in a close relationship with someone who hurts us unfairly, we may question our "just world view." In other words, we may wonder if our beliefs about what is just or fair are accurate, or if other people have vastly different beliefs than our own. As a result, we may have to alter our personal views or at least accept the fact that some people live their lives according to quite different rules of fairness.

A man who has been hurt by the abortion decision of his partner may believe that not only his partner, but also society has violated his view of justice. I would have to agree with him given our current laws concerning abortion. Expectant fathers are not equally or fairly protected under the law. However, if a man fears that all women are like his partner, he is making a global judgment based on the behavior of a single woman.

All women do not support legalized abortion and, of those that do, all do not agree that the decision to abort should rest solely with the woman. While some people would agree that men have been treated unfairly, others would not. Even as the post-abortion man accepts that not all people share his beliefs, he doesn't have to compromise those beliefs. He can maintain his "just world view" in spite of the fact that others may, on occasion, threaten it.

In addition to dealing with the threat to his view of justice, the post-abortion man also must deal with the pain resulting from the loss of a relationship. If his pain is not dealt with, it may well prevent or sabotage future relationships. When a post-abortion man enters into a new relationship with anger and low expectations of his new partner, he is likely to behave in ways that practically ensure another failed relationship. His inappropriate expression of pain toward an innocent target can only result in the perpetuation of pain for himself and injury to another who doesn't deserve it. Only when the post-abortion man makes a deliberate decision to work through his pain, will he become capable of building a healthy relationship with another. Again, I am not talking about denying or minimizing pain, but rather admitting it and willfully choosing to avoid passing it on to others.

Ultimately, forgiveness requires us to face reality and accept the fact that people sometimes behave imperfectly and unfairly. We all fail at times and behave in ways that violate our faith or personal code. As we forgive those who have failed us, we need to accept the fact that some people do not share our view of justice. This understanding may help us to choose future partners more carefully. When we forgive and choose to control our pain, we reduce the risk of misdirecting our anger toward others. Then, when we enter into new relationships, our expectations won't be distorted by bad experiences with people from our past.

Knowing that we can forgive and survive if we are hurt again also helps us to feel a sense of control. This regained sense of control serves to decrease anxiety about relationships. Finally, without forgiveness there can be no reconciliation with one's partner or perhaps with women in general.

Because relationships give meaning to our lives, fear of relationships can result in isolation and depression. Given the importance of our relationships, it makes sense to do what we must to maintain them. Forgiveness is essential in order to both preserve current relationships and to enable us to pursue future relationships with confidence.

Putting the Ideas into Practice

Acknowledge your fear and accept that it is normal and healthy following a deep hurt. Fear can be a survival signal letting us know when we may be in danger. It can motivate us to back away from and reevaluate that which threatens us.

As one means to gain some control over your fear, pay attention to your thoughts and ask yourself the following questions:

1. How often do I find myself feeling frightened?
2. When do I seem most likely to feel fear? (When I'm away from home? When I'm meeting someone new? When I'm with a woman?)
3. How do I experience fear? (my pulse races, I can't seem to speak clearly...)

You can use your answers to the questions to help you conquer your fear by doing the following:

1. Think of some positive statements that you can say to yourself whenever you are feeling fearful. For example, if you are afraid that you can't trust *any* woman, tell yourself that "not *all* women are the same and not *all* of them are untrustworthy." For positive self-talk to work, you have to believe in the logic of your statement.
2. If you are going to be in a situation which you know may intensify your fear, do what you can to alter it. For example, if meeting a new woman is frightening, try to do so in a group setting where you will have plenty of other familiar people nearby.
3. If you are experiencing physical manifestations of fear, practice slowing your breathing. This requires a con-

scious focus as you slowly breathe in and slowly exhale. If you believe you may be experiencing anxiety attacks, a medical evaluation may be necessary.

Make a list of the qualities or characteristics you would use to describe an ideal relationship. Of course, no relationship is perfect, but many relationships are good. Your list is a starting point where you begin to consider the qualities you want to work on in a new relationship.

Remind yourself that relationships give our lives meaning but they will always involve a certain amount of risk. If you want to experience the joys of relationships, then you have to be willing to risk the pain.

Forgiving the one who hurt you enables you to enter into a new relationship without a lot of emotional baggage. Forgiveness frees you from the past and prevents your past from sabotaging your future.

Paul's Story

PAUL AND JULIE WERE IN their early twenties when they married. Both had hopes for a happy future together in spite of some problems in their relationship. During the first year of their marriage, Julie became pregnant. After seeing a doctor, she decided to obtain an abortion. Paul described his reaction to her decision at the time as "indifferent."

Julie had the abortion and Paul told me, "I'll never forget the look on her face, she was crying and shaking." In spite of her obvious emotional distress, Paul said, "We never talked about the abortion, not in nine years of marriage." They literally never discussed it. Nine years later, he and Julie were divorced.

After the divorce, Paul was involved in other relationships but he never remarried. He found himself often taking the role of "nurturer" in these relationships as he believed that role to be safer than allowing himself to be dependent on another. In hindsight, he also may have been attempting to atone for his perceived failure with Julie. As he said, "I was her husband, I was her protector, I was her provider, and I let this [the abortion] happen to her."

In contrast to his need to be nurturing of others, Paul was engaging in very self-destructive behaviors, including alcohol and drug abuse, after the divorce. He also experienced difficulty getting emotionally close to women and said, "It was kind of a self-punishment, like I didn't believe I deserved to have a healthy relationship."

Paul realized some time later that his behavior was symptomatic of underlying grief and guilt. This realization occurred after he became a Christian. When I met Paul, he was aware that he was still struggling with grief, guilt, and anger at the doctor who recommended abortion. He was interested in working through these emotions and closing a painful chapter of his life.

Paul already knew that God had forgiven him. He was sure of God's forgiveness but still wasn't able to forgive himself. He was also concerned that he hadn't truly forgiven the doctor. His grief was due to multiple losses; he had lost a wife, a child, and his sense of self-worth.

I met Paul 22 years after his abortion experience. That's a very long time to carry such a heavy burden. Eventually, Paul was able to work through his grief and to forgive both the doctor and himself. He will always regret his part in the abortion but he no longer suffers from self-condemnation and overwhelming grief. Paul believes that his experience has made him less judgmental of other people and more tender-hearted toward them. He continues to use his experience to minister to others.

Chapter Nine

GRIEF AND FORGIVENESS

GRIEF IS A NORMAL RESPONSE to a significant loss. It may be experienced emotionally, cognitively, and/or behaviorally. For example, the emotional signs of grief could include feelings of sadness, helplessness, even anger. Cognitive symptoms of grief may be evidenced by an inability to concentrate or persistent thoughts about the loss. The physical or behavioral expression of grief may be experienced as a decrease in energy or appetite or in sleep disturbances.

The intensity of one's grief is related to the perceived significance of that which has been lost. A man who has experienced an abortion may be dealing with multiple losses. He may be grieving for the loss of his child, the loss of his relationship with his partner, and the loss of his dreams for the future. He may even be grieving over the loss of his self-image. The following comments were made by the men who participated in our research:

"Abortion is a loss, no question about it!"

"It's not really something tangible, it's a loss of an idea or a possibility to a man."

"Sure it was her body, but it [the baby] was a part of me."

"Here was this person I loved and I thought I'd finally have my family. Now I lost that person, that child, and that family."

"I'll never be able to forget that child, the child that I lost."

Several of the men observed that their grief was intensified at certain times of the year. They reported increased feelings of sadness at the time of year when the abortion occurred and/or said that they felt particularly down during the month when the baby was due to be born. All of them experienced significant grief following their losses and most of them said that they were grieving over multiple losses including loss of the child, the relationship, and their self-esteem.

It is notable that, when discussing their abortion experiences, none of the men referred to their loss as a "fetus." Each of them referred to their lost children as "my baby" or "my child." They did not separate the physiological condition of pregnancy from the developing child. They believed that abortion ended a human life that was precious to them. In fact, many of them talked about how old their children would be had they lived.

The majority of the men in our study were in serious relationships with their partners and, for them, the end of a meaningful relationship was another major loss to grieve. They lost women they deeply cared for as well as their dreams for the future.

These men also suffered a loss of self-esteem. They felt that they had failed to protect their children and/or their partners. They saw themselves as having failed as men. Many of them viewed the abortion as a personal rejection.

Some of the men observed that their grief did not become apparent until quite some time after the abortion occurred. These men said that they were more aware of feeling angry than sad. They believed that their anger was a deliberate, although perhaps subconscious, attempt to hide their grief. As one of the research volunteers stated, "After the abortion, it started a downhill slide for me. I engaged in a lot of self-destructive behaviors. I acted angry but there was grief there." This man's comment serves to illustrate one of the factors which may make the post-abortion man's resolution of grief more difficult. That is that many men prefer to feel and express anger rather than grief because grief may be perceived as an emotion of weakness.

Some men may not get in touch with their own feelings until long after the abortion because, at the time of the actual abortion, they were preoccupied with supporting their partners. This too can complicate the grieving process. When such a man finally experiences grief, he may be puzzled about feeling sad so long after the event. Because of the time lapse, he may not connect his grief with the actual abortion.

Another factor which may complicate the post-abortion man's resolution of grief is society's lack of validation of his grief. Since society does not recognize and validate the man's loss, he may be confused about why he feels the way he does and how he ought to deal with his feelings. He may even be unaware that his negative emotions, such as anger or sadness, are related to a previous abortion experience.

Given these factors which may make it difficult to complete the grieving process, I would encourage a man who has been hurt by abortion to do the following: First, he should try to take an objective view of his thoughts, feelings, and behaviors. He may find himself frequently thinking about his loss, even obsessing about it. On the other hand, he may not consciously think about the abortion at all unless his memory is triggered by certain events (e.g. being around infants or small children, experiencing a future pregnancy). It is also useful for him to determine if he is feeling intense anger or sadness. His anger may be a cover for underlying sadness. Of course, a man may experience both of these emotions at the same time. Anger may lead him to engage in self-destructive behaviors while sadness may make it difficult for him to get through each day. If he is experiencing difficulty with the daily tasks of living or if he has had suicidal thoughts since the abortion, then it is imperative that he seek counseling. When grief is not resolved, it can lead to depression and despair.

Second, it is very important for the post-abortion man to express his grief. I cannot overemphasize the importance of this. Those who have suffered from abortion need to actively grieve their loss. For most of us, grieving includes shedding tears. Many years ago, I read about a study concerning different types of tears. It has been so long now that I can no longer remember the source of this research but I do remember the results. The investigators discovered that tears that were due to either irritation of the eyes, or sadness, or laughter were different in chemical make-up. In other words, the tears we cry when we are feeling sad are really different from those we cry when we are laughing hard or peeling onions. That suggests that crying may provide us with more than just psychological relief.

Another essential way for the post-abortion man to express his grief is by talking with a sympathetic person about his abortion experience. All of the men who participated in this research said that they found it difficult to talk to others about their personal abortion experiences. Some, like Paul, never even discussed it with their partners after the abortion was over. The men identified a number of reasons for this difficulty such as the personal nature of the topic, the pain of recalling the incident, and the fear of being condemned. I asked them what they would say to other men who have been hurt by abortion and they made the following comments:

> "It's okay to feel the way you feel... this is the first thing you have to deal with. It's okay to feel cheated."
>
> "It's okay to feel the way you do... denial, grief, anger, sadness, depression are all a part of it."
>
> "I realized you can't do that, keep things inside and not express your feelings."

These men recognized the necessity of accepting and expressing their feelings. Of course, it would be counterproductive for the post-abortion man to speak with someone who can't appreciate the depth of his loss and pain or someone who is likely to make him feel more guilty than he already does. I would encourage him to carefully choose a confidante who is likely to respond to him with empathy and compassion. For those men who are hesitant to speak with someone they know, they might try contacting a local crisis pregnancy center. These centers frequently have counselors and/or structured programs for both post-abortion men and women.

There are counselors and therapists who are trained to

deal with grief issues and some even focus on what has come to be referred to as "Post-Abortion Syndrome."[1,2,3,4] This syndrome has been discussed primarily in terms of women but abortion has been recognized as being traumatic for men as well.[5,6] The symptoms of Post-Abortion Syndrome may include the following: recurrent thoughts or dreams concerning the abortion or the lost child, a decreased interest in significant relationships and activities, hostility toward others or the self, difficulty concentrating, guilt, grief, anxiety, decreased self-esteem, self-condemnation, sexual dysfunction, and even suicidal thoughts.[7,8,9] The symptoms of Post-Abortion Syndrome may not be evident until months or even years after the abortion actually occurred. Some of the events that may trigger symptoms include anniversary dates of either the abortion or the expected due date, and also future pregnancies.

Several of the men I worked with stated that they experienced recurrent and intrusive thoughts concerning the abortion and the lost child. Some also reported insomnia, unpleasant dreams related to the abortion, sexual dysfunction, isolation, inability to concentrate, hostility, anxiety, guilt, depression, and lowered self-esteem. Given the magnitude of their loss, this is not surprising. However, the grief following an abortion can be dealt with and processed just as grief following any other loss can be. In the case of abortion though, it is critical that the man seek out an individual who will validate his experience. It is my hope that this information will help post-abortion men to recognize that their experience is normal and to motivate them to seek some form of support whether it be from a close friend, family member, clergy, or a professional counselor.

In addition to finding a supportive person to share his experience with, I would suggest an exercise which the men in our study completed. I asked each of them to answer the following question: "What good has or could possibly come out of your grief?" The purpose of this exercise was to instill hope and alleviate grief by finding meaning in a very painful experience. All of the men were able to answer this question in spite of the fact that none of them ever wanted to endure another abortion. One of the men stated that his experience caused him to realize as never before that "Life is the most precious thing to us because it's the only thing we have." Another man said that "One of the good things about grief is that you get rid of your cocky attitude. You realize that the small things really don't matter." Still another stated that, "People who honestly go through a grieving process can better help other people." None of the men wished to experience another abortion but all of them were able to view their experiences as valuable learning opportunities. This enabled them to extract meaning from their painful past and to begin to think about how it might positively impact their future.

The discovery of meaning in a hurtful event is one of the components or steps in the forgiveness process. The fact that finding meaning is a healthy part of both forgiveness and grief resolution implies a possible connection between these two psychological processes. Forgiveness and grief resolution are related in the sense that forgiveness can help us to resolve our grief when our grief is due to a serious injury caused by another or by ourselves.

Finding meaning in our suffering may enable us to at least begin to feel more hopeful about the future. The fact that forgiveness is an active (although internal) process also may foster a renewed sense of hope. This may be, in part, because doing something often seems to make us feel better than doing nothing. When we choose to forgive the one who has hurt us, we choose to make an active response toward that person. We are, in effect, doing something about our situation with the hope that both we and those who have hurt us can let go of the past and look forward to the future.

There is another step in the forgiveness process which may help with grief resolution. That step involves absorption of the pain that has been suffered. Recall that this requires a conscious decision to deliberately avoid passing our pain on to innocent others. In order to do this, the man will need to make an honest appraisal of his injury. This is a necessary step in grief resolution as well as in forgiveness. Neither of these processes can be completed if the injured person denies or represses reality. Grief must be acknowledged, expressed, and worked through if it is to be resolved. Because abortion results in permanent consequences, the post-abortion man may always carry some residual grief and regret. Nonetheless, if he chooses to share his grief with an empathetic person and also to avoid displacing his pain on to others, he will avoid creating more grief for himself and others.

The post-abortion man may be better able to forgive his partner if he considers the fact that she also may be grieving. Remember, Post-Abortion Syndrome was first identified as a disorder affecting post-abortion women. It took nearly two decades of legalized abortion before this syndrome was recognized. Women, as well as men, have not had their grief validated as being socially acceptable. In addition, the man's partner actually endured the abortion procedure. She has experienced both the physical and psychological consequences of abortion.

All of the men who took part in our research demonstrated significant gains in forgiveness toward their partners.

Of those who indicated that self-forgiveness was an issue they wanted to work on, all evidenced significant gains in self-forgiveness. Each of the men also demonstrated significant reductions in grief. It would appear then that the decision to forgive themselves and the ones who hurt them was beneficial in terms of alleviating their grief. While a post-abortion man may always experience some degree of sadness when he is reminded of his loss, forgiveness can bring an appreciable reduction in his grief.

For some, grief reduction may be further facilitated by a ritual or concrete symbol of the loss. For example, some people have chosen to have a priest or pastor perform a ceremony in which the lost child is remembered and consecrated. There have also been memorials established to commemorate children lost through abortion. These are actual sites which post-abortion men and women can visit in order to acknowledge and honor their children. Some men I know have written poems for their lost children or letters to them.

A reminder of God's love for little children also may be comforting. In the gospel of Mark, we read that people were bringing their children to Jesus in the hope that He would touch them. The disciples were annoyed by this and rebuked them. "When Jesus saw this, He was indignant. He said to His disciples, 'Let the little children come to me, and do not hinder them, for the kingdom of God belongs to such as these....' And He took the children in His arms, put His hands on them and blessed them."[10] Scriptures such as these may provide comfort to bereaved parents and also the assurance that their children are at peace with the Lord. Those men who believe that their children are with God have the additional hope that they will someday be reunited and reconciled with them.

As the post-abortion man's grief lessens, he will experience a renewal of joy and hope. The late Henri Nouwen, priest and author, has written that, "There is an intimate relationship between joy and hope. While optimism makes us live as if someday soon things will go better for us, hope frees us from the need to predict the future and allows us to live in the present, with the deep trust that God will never leave us alone but will fulfill the deepest desires of our heart. Joy in this perspective is the fruit of hope."[11] As the post-abortion man travels on the convergent paths of forgiveness and grief resolution, he can confidently face both his present and his future with hope and joy.

Putting the Ideas into Practice

Acknowledge your grief and accept that it is normal. Although many in our society still do not recognize post-abortion grief as valid, hundreds of thousands of men and women will attest to the fact that abortion entails a very painful loss. Those who have experienced suicidal thoughts after an abortion *must* seek professional help.

Remember that anger may be a cover for underlying grief. Consider the possibility that you may be *acting* angry but *feeling* sad.

Express your grief in one or more of the following ways:

1. Allow yourself to cry.
2. Speak to an empathetic and trusted listener (friend, parent, clergyperson, or counselor) about your sadness.
3. Express your grief in a concrete manner that makes your lost child more tangible by...
   - naming your child
   - writing a poem about or a letter to your child
   - building or planting something in your child's honor
   - asking a clergyman to conduct a service for your child
   - visiting one of the memorials around the country which have been established to honor the children lost by abortion
   - donating a memorial stone, honoring aborted children, to a local cemetery

In order to find meaning in your suffering, ask yourself the following questions:

1. "What have I learned from this experience?"
2. "What good could possibly come out of my suffering?"

Share your answers to these questions with others who are grieving so that you might help them to find meaning also.

The processes of forgiveness and grief resolution are similar in that both entail a loss and a struggle to find meaning in one's suffering. As you forgive the one who hurt you and also grieve your loss, you can find meaning in your pain. Finding meaning lessens your grief and increases your hope. When you have hope, *anything* is possible!

David's Story

DAVID WAS 19 AND HIS girlfriend, Jill, was 18 when she became pregnant. David and Jill had been dating for two years; he was working full-time and she was in her last year of high school. Both of them believed that their relationship was serious and that they would marry after Jill graduated.

David recalled feeling "terrified" when Jill told him that she was pregnant. David told me that they didn't consider alternatives to abortion because "abortion seemed easier than telling our parents or dealing with all of the responsibilities." The decision was mutual and seemed to be their only option.

According to David, shortly after the abortion, "things got rocky and then they got worse." He and Jill argued frequently and their physical relationship was no longer satisfying. In fact, both started "sleeping around with other people." David described himself as feeling "detached, dead, and confused" after the abortion. He said, "I drank to avoid thinking about it. I got very promiscuous after the abortion. The more sex I got, the worse I felt about myself." He and Jill couldn't or wouldn't discuss the abortion and eventually their relationship ended.

David is now 32 years old. He has shared his experience with close friends and with his pastor and all have been supportive of him. He feels at peace with God and has also forgiven himself.

At this time, David is actively involved with a Christian youth ministry. He is very much aware of the fears and temptations which teenagers face and he has used his experience to both warn and encourage them. He is very concerned that widespread abortion has "desensitized" people. His work with adolescents is his way of using the lessons he has learned to help others.

When I asked David to tell me what message he would most like to share with others, this is what he said:

> "I wish society would look at the long-term effects [of abortion] on both men and women so they could see the long-term damage it does to people. Then they could inform and warn people before the abortion, or better yet, before the pregnancy."

Chapter Ten

HELPING OTHERS TO HEAL

AN IMPORTANT PART OF the healing process is helping others to heal. The post-abortion man who has experienced healing is in a unique position to help other men who have been hurt by abortion. Like David, all of the men I worked with listed 'prevention' as one of the most important ways they could help other men. Some, like David, emphasized pregnancy prevention by abstaining from sex outside of marriage. Others emphasized birth control and all stressed the importance of warning a man about the potential psychological consequences following abortion. None of these men were prepared for the magnitude of their pain because the abortion option has been presented as a benign medical procedure.

Who better than a man who has been deeply hurt by a personal abortion experience fully understands the painful emotions of anger, helplessness, guilt, and grief and, the difficulty in sharing those feelings with others? He is also acutely aware of how an abortion can affect a man's relationships with other people and with God. His experience of both pain and subsequent healing provide him with the knowledge to minister to other men.

Some men may choose to acquire some form of training in order to function as professional or volunteer counselors for other post-abortion men. Others may choose to put their efforts into legislation to protect fathers' rights and/or those of unborn children. Still others, like David, may choose to educate young men about the dangers of sex in a relationship that lacks commitment. Most men will simply make themselves 'available' to others. By that I mean that they will forever carry a sensitivity to and empathy for other post-abortion men which will enable them to facilitate the healing of those other men.

It would be useful for all post-abortion men to remember that simply listening to others has powerful therapeutic effects. All of the men in this study identified 'listening' as a means by which they could help other post-abortion men. Active listening requires that the one who is listening devote his full attention to the one speaking. He allows the speaker to share his most private and painful thoughts for as long as necessary. Sometimes, it may seem that the one sharing his abortion experience is confused or repetitive. This is a normal part of 'processing' or working through a painful experience. It takes time to absorb the reality of the experience and to sort out both blame and emotions. Being allowed to take his time as he expresses himself will help the post-abortion man to work through his experience.

It is especially important to validate his experience and to assure him that it is normal. Other men have also experienced intense emotions (e.g. anger, guilt, grief), nightmares, frequent thoughts about the abortion or the baby, difficulty concentrating, relationship and/or sexual problems, fear of punishment, and increased risk-taking behaviors. While each man's experience is unique, available data suggest that these symptoms or problems are not unusual. A man needs to be assured that he is not abnormal in terms of his response to the abortion.

At the same time, it is important to remind him that there is hope. That is, he can be healed and able to look to the future with a renewed sense of confidence. The healing journey will not be easy but it is necessary if he is to find relief. A list of post-abortion resources may be found in Appendix C. These resources include various healing ministries as well as organizations that can provide referrals within a requested geographic area. Men may find considerable help in their healing process by contacting one of these resource agencies. Men who have already experienced healing may want to contact one of these organizations in order to find out how they can become more involved in facilitating the healing of others.

After a period of listening and validating, it may be time to encourage the post-abortion man to seek forgiveness from those he has harmed and to offer forgiveness to those who have hurt him. Some may be eager to pursue forgiveness while others may need more time to work through their anger. The listener needs to be sensitive to the other's readiness to forgive. Even after the man makes a commitment to forgive, he may need to be reminded that giving and receiving forgiveness can be difficult and he needs to be gentle and patient with both himself and others. The heart doesn't always work as quickly as the head. He may need to be reassured that it is normal to struggle with negative emotions toward himself or others even while he has more positive thoughts.

When approaching the topic of forgiveness, it is imperative that the difference between excusing and forgiving be made clear. A man who is feeling very angry toward a partner who chose abortion against his wishes needs to understand that he can forgive his partner even while he blames her. After all, had she done nothing wrong, there would be nothing to forgive. It may be helpful to explain the concept of reframing to him so that he can see his partner in a larger context (that is, as a fellow human being who struggles with fear and confusion). Similarly, the man who seems overwhelmed with self-condemnation may be hesitant to seek forgiveness or forgive himself unless his guilt is validated and he is encouraged to reframe his view of himself. As he is helped to see himself as prone to moral failure just as every other human is, he may be more receptive to receiving God's forgiveness as well as forgiving himself.

While a post-abortion man may always carry some sadness and regret, he can be helped to bear any residual pain. Scripture references, particularly those dealing with God's gift of forgiveness, His promise of eternal life, and His love for children may be shared with him. If he can accept the assurance of God's forgiveness and believe in God's expressed love for his unborn child, he will be relieved of the paralyzing emotions of guilt and despair. Instead, he can live his life with the assurance of his own worth and with the assurance that someday he will be reunited with his child. This assurance will enable him to demonstrate compassion toward others as well as toward himself.

For the non-believer, a concrete gesture may be especially helpful. He may find comfort in doing something concrete to honor his lost child such as naming the child, visiting a memorial site dedicated to the unborn, or establishing his own memorial (e.g. a planting, a poem, or a stone dedicated to the child).

As one post-abortion man helps another, both are healed and made whole again. Now, instead of one, there are two who are equipped to minister to still other men. As more and more men become willing to share their experience and the lessons they have learned, the number of potential ministers will be vastly multiplied. The exponential growth in such a ministry could have a profound and beneficial impact on hundreds of thousands of men.

When healing is shared, people find meaning in living and in suffering. The late psychiatrist, Viktor Frankl, believed that "man's main concern is not to gain pleasure or to avoid pain but rather to see a meaning in his life."[1] He claimed that "life's meaning is an unconditional one" and that "unconditional meaning is paralleled by the unconditional value of each and every person."[2] Frankl was saying that life has meaning and people have value in spite of their circumstances. Given the fact that Frankl was a survivor of a concentration camp and lost all but a sister in the camps, his optimistic philosophy is quite remarkable. In spite of his personal suffering, he found meaning in his existence and subsequently developed a treatment approach called "logotherapy" to help others do the same.

I believe that men who have been hurt by abortion can find healing and meaning through forgiveness. They may do so by offering forgiveness to those who have hurt them, by receiving forgiveness from those they have wronged, and finally by forgiving themselves. Post-abortion men who have found healing and meaning through forgiveness can be a blessing to many. As they share this healing with others, all are more able to appreciate and celebrate the precious gift of life.

"What a wonderful God we have, He is the Father of our Lord Jesus Christ, the source of every mercy, and the one who so wonderfully comforts and strengthens us in our hardships and trials. And why does He do this? So that when others are troubled, needing our sympathy and encouragement, we can pass on to them this same help and comfort God has given us" (2 Corinthians 1:3-4).

Putting the Ideas into Practice

Trust in your ability to help others. Your experience has taught you valuable lessons that you can share.

Make yourself available to those who are hurting. You can do this by practicing active listening. Active listening requires that you give the speaker your full attention. Focus on really hearing what the speaker is saying; don't be distracted by thinking about how you will respond to him.

Be a patient listener as he sorts out his feelings. His grief and confusion may make it difficult for him to articulate what he is feeling. If you are comfortable when he pauses to find the right words, you will be giving him permission to move at his own pace.

Accept and validate his feelings and his story. His experience may not sound exactly like your own and you may be tempted to give advice too soon.

Share your own experience *after* he has had a chance to share his. The purpose of sharing your experience is to let him know that his pain and grief are normal.

Let him know that there is hope and that healing is possible. Tell him that healing will take time and require a good deal of work on his part but you will be there to help him.

Gently approach the topic of forgiveness when he seems ready to discuss it. Often, people are more willing to consider forgiving another after they have expressed their anger. An effective way to discuss forgiveness may be for you to share your own struggle to forgive and the healing you received after you completed the forgiveness process.

Remind him of God's love and His desire to forgive all who ask for His forgiveness. He can know this forgiveness and be free of guilt and shame.

Encourage him by telling him that as he is healed, he will be able to help still others to find healing. As he does so, he will be bringing good out of his painful past.

Appendix A

Testing a Healing Program for Post-Abortion Men

CLINICAL INTERVENTION research is carried out in order to determine if a therapeutic program is useful in terms of helping a specific group of people to find healing. When investigators want to determine if an intervention program will be successful, they form two groups of participants referred to as the "experimental" and "control" groups. The experimental group receives the experimental treatment while the control group receives either no treatment or a placebo. Then the researchers compare the groups to determine if there are significant differences between them. When statistically significant differences favoring the experimental group are found, it can be said that the intervention appeared to be effective.

Volunteers for our study were obtained through a newspaper advertisement which read, "Adult males needed for research concerning men who have been hurt by abortion." Thus, the men who responded to the ad identified themselves as having been hurt by an abortion experience. This is an important point because we began the research with the assumption that some men have been hurt by abortion. We did not assume that all men suffered greatly after an abortion experience and we wanted to limit our study to only those men who identified themselves as having been hurt. After the men responded to the advertisement, they were screened via an interview to determine if they were still having problems related to the abortion and if they could identify one person, other than themselves, whom they most blamed for the abortion.

Finding volunteers for clinical research is always challenging. Finding post-abortion men who are willing to speak about their experience is an additional challenge. There are a number of reasons why men may be hesitant to discuss an abortion experience.

First, some men may be in denial. In other words, they may not yet have faced the fact that the abortion hurt them. They may be totally unaware that they are angry, anxious, depressed, or feeling guilty. Men who have an abortion in their past and who are having difficulty concentrating, experiencing angry outbursts, exhibiting signs of grief, and are fearful of relationships might consider that these may be symptoms of an unresolved abortion experience.

Unresolved anger and guilt following an abortion also may contribute to reckless behavior such as drug and alcohol abuse or sexual promiscuity. Obviously, the men who responded to our ad were beyond denial and well aware of their post-abortion pain. Second, I have observed what others have reported and that is a genuine desire on the man's part to support his female partner by containing his own emotions. Rather than expressing his own pain or seeking help for himself, the man may believe that his primary responsibility is to help his partner. A third factor which may contribute to the man's inclination to avoid discussing his experience is our society's socialization process for males. In spite of the changing roles and expectations of men and women, there is still a great deal of pressure on men to maintain a strong and controlled front. Society's portrayal of abortion as a woman's issue may be another reason that men tend not to talk about their abortion experiences. Because of this portrayal, there is nearly a total lack of recognition by society that men should feel anything related to abortion. It is extremely difficult for people to express grief and work through grief when they are given the message that their grief is not valid. Finally, there is the privacy factor. Both men and women would be expected to avoid talking about an issue as personal and private as that of abortion.

Of the men who did respond to the advertisement, only about half of them were determined to be eligible for our study. Some of the respondents lived too far away or were not planning on being in the immediate area long enough to participate in the program. One man was dealing with the loss of a grandchild and we decided to limit this research to only men who lost an immediate child. Another man claimed to be having only sexual problems following his wife's abortion and we were focusing on emotional problems. Still another man was eliminated because he knew too much about the intervention goal even before the research was begun and his knowledge could have biased our results.

The group of men who eventually participated in this study ranged in age from 21 to 43 years. All of them were single upon starting the program and one married during the study. Two of them had one living child. While the majority of the volunteers (60%) identified themselves as

Christian, one was Muslim and the rest described themselves as agnostic. Half of the volunteers were opposed to their partners' abortions from the time they learned of the pregnancies. One of the men was supportive initially and one was not told of the abortion until months after the procedure. The rest of the men described themselves as feeling ambivalent and/or confused at the time the decision to abort was made. A majority of the men had been through a single abortion experience while three of them experienced two abortions each. None of the men were still in relationships with their partners who obtained abortions. The time span between the men's abortion experience and contact with myself ranged from six months to 22 years.

These volunteers were randomly assigned to either the treatment or control group. All of the men knew that they might be working on the treatment program with the experimenter immediately or that they might have to wait 12 weeks to begin the program. As I said previously, usually those in the control group receive either no treatment or a placebo. We felt strongly that we were ethically obligated to offer the program to both groups.

Before any of the men began the program, all of them were given measures to assess their levels of anger, anxiety, and grief. In addition, they were asked to complete a survey which measured how much they had forgiven the person they most blamed for the abortion. The words "anger," "anxiety," "grief," and "forgiveness" were not on the surveys so while the men could guess what we were measuring, they didn't actually know. This is standard procedure in research as it is one means to increase the accuracy of responses. This first assessment is called the pre-test. The purpose is to obtain information concerning the individual's psychological state before he takes part in the treatment program. A measure of forgiveness was used because the goal of the intervention program was to foster forgiveness. Previous research has indicated that forgiveness promotes psychological healing.[1,2,3] The other surveys utilized were chosen because they measured some of the areas which may be problematic for post-abortion men. We hypothesized that as the men became more forgiving, they would also evidence less anger, anxiety, and grief. Thus, the decision to forgive would be realized in improved psychological health.

After the pre-tests were completed, the men assigned to the experimental group began the program. I met individually with each experimental participant for 12 weekly sessions. Each session lasted approximately 90 minutes. At the first session, the participant was told that the goal of the intervention program was to facilitate forgiveness of the person he most blamed for the abortion other than himself. A secondary goal of the program was to foster self-forgiveness if the man was struggling with guilt. None of the men knew that forgiveness was the goal of the program until the first intervention session. This is important because, had anyone known about the goal prior to beginning the program, it could have biased our results. In scientific experiments, it is critical to try to maintain control over all factors that could influence your results. We wanted to ensure that we were testing the effectiveness of the actual program and not the effectiveness of the men just thinking about forgiveness.

After the program was completed with the men in the experimental group, all of the men (experimental and control participants) were given the first post-test. This included the same measures used for the pre-test. We were hoping that the men assigned to the experimental group would show improvement on these measures since they had now completed the program and that the men in the control group would appear to be the same since they had simply been in a waiting period for 12 weeks. This is exactly what we found. The experimental group appeared to be more forgiving and less angry, anxious, and sad than the men who had still not been through the program. Also, the men in the experimental group, who stated that they were having difficulty forgiving themselves, now appeared to be significantly more self-forgiving.

Next, the men assigned to the control group met with me on an individual basis for 12 weekly sessions and when we completed the treatment program, all of the men were given the second post-test. The same measures were used and again, the men who had now participated in the program appeared to be more forgiving and less angry, anxious, and sad than they were previously. The men in the control group also appeared to have become more forgiving of themselves following the intervention. In addition, the experimental group appeared to be maintaining that which had been gained from the program. In other words, 12 weeks after they finished the program, the men in the experimental group were still demonstrating increased forgiveness and a decrease in anger, anxiety, grief, and guilt just as they did immediately after the intervention.

Prior to participating in the intervention program, these men told me that they were experiencing various problems since the abortion. All of the men stated that they experienced sadness, difficulty concentrating, anger, and guilt. Relationship problems and helplessness were the two areas that the men identified as those they struggled with most frequently. Also, the majority of men stated that they felt confused about the male's role in society. After the research was completed, both the survey results and comments from the men indicated improvement in these areas.

The men who volunteered for this study made many comments about feeling better and feeling satisfied that they had made the choice to participate. All of the men were told initially that they could drop out of the study at any time for any reason. None of them chose to do so. Each of the men expressed the hope that, by taking part in our research, he would be helping other men who have been hurt by an abortion experience. I cannot thank them enough. I have learned a great deal from each of them and that knowledge will hopefully benefit other men.

Appendix B

PROCESSES OF FORGIVING ANOTHER

Uncovering Phase

1. Examination of psychological defenses (Kiel, 1986).
2. Confrontation of anger; the point is to release, not harbor, the anger (Trainer, 1981).
3. Admittance of shame, when this is appropriate (Patton, 1985).
4. Awareness of cathexis (Droll, 1984).
5. Awareness of cognitive rehearsal of the offense (Droll, 1984).
6. Insight that the injured party may be comparing self with the injurer (Kiel, 1986).
7. Realization that oneself may be permanently and adversely changed by the injury (Close, 1970).
8. Insight into a possibly altered "just world" view (Flanigan, 1987).

Decision Phase

9. A change of heart, conversion, new insights that old resolution strategies are not working (North, 1987).
10. Willingness to consider forgiveness as an option.
11. Commitment to forgive the offender (Neblett, 1974).

Work Phase

12. Reframing, through role-taking, who the wrongdoer is by viewing him or her in context (Smith, 1981).
13. Empathy toward the offender (Cunningham, 1985).
14. Compassion toward the offender (Droll, 1984).
15. Acceptance, absorption of the pain (Bergin, 1988).

Outcome or Deepening Phase

16. Finding meaning for self and others in the suffering and in the forgiveness process (Frankl, 1959).
17. Realization that self has needed others' forgiveness in the past (Cunningham, 1985).
18. Insight that one is not alone (universality, support).
19. Realization that self may have a new purpose in life because of the injury.
20. Awareness of decreased negative affect and, perhaps, increased positive affect, if this begins to emerge, toward the injurer; awareness of internal emotional release (Smedes, 1984).

Note: This table is an extrapolation from and extension of Enright and the Human Development Study Group (1991). The references at the end of each unit are prototypical examples or discussions of that unit.

Appendix C

Post-Abortion Resources

National Office of Post-Abortion Reconciliation and Healing
P.O. Box 07077
Milwaukee, WI 53207-0477
Phone: (414) 483-4141 or (800) 5WE-CARE (593-2273)
(Provides referrals for counseling and training in post-abortion counseling) www.marquette.edu/rachel

Institute for Pregnancy Loss
P.O. Box 279
37 Depot Road
Stratham, NH 03885
Phone: (603) 778-1450

Care Net
109 Carpenter Drive/Suite 100
Sterling, VA 20164
Phone: (703) 478-5661

(Care Net has counseling centers all across the U.S. and can provide referrals upon request.) www.care-net.org

Heartbeat International
665 E. Dublin-Granville Road Suite 40
Columbus, OH 43229
Phone: (614) 885-7577
www.heartbeatinternational.org

MARC Ministries/Men's Abortion Recovery
Dr. Wayne Brauning
237 S. 13th Avenue
Coatesville, PA 19320
Phone: (610) 384-3210

The Elliot Institute
P.O. Box 7348
Springfield, IL 62791
www.afterabortion.org
(The Elliot Institute publishes *The Post-Abortion Review* quarterly. The institute engages in both research and education concerning the effects of abortion.)

New Life Family Services
1515 E. 66th Street
Richfield, MN 55423
Phone: (612) 866-7643 or (612) 866-7715
(24-hour hotline)
www.newlifefamilyservices.com

Fathers and Brothers Ministries
777 Panorama Court
Boulder, CO 80303
Phone: (303) 543-0148
e-mail: warrenlwil@aol.com

Healing Hearts Ministry
Grace Kern, Director
2717 York Road
Oak Brook, IL 60523
Phone: (630) 990-0909 or (888) 217-8679

Victims of Choice
P.O. Box 815
Naperville, IL 60566-0815
Phone: (630) 378-1680 or (888) 267-3998
www.victimsofchoice.org
email: eav@victimsofchoice.org

National Memorial for the Unborn
6230 Vance Road
Chatanooga, TN 37421
Phone: (800) 505-5565
www.memorial-unborn.org
e-mail: mail@memorial-unborn.net

Websites:

1) www.abortionresearch.net

This site includes a survey which was developed to collect data concerning the effects of abortion on men. Questions and/or comments may be e-mailed to: ctcoyle@hotmail.com

2) www.marquette.edu/rachel

This site contains helpful information about the aftermath of abortion and also lists Project Rachel centers throughout the U.S. which offer post-abortion counseling.

3) www.prolifeinfo.org

This is the most comprehensive listing of prolife information including that related to politics, abortion alternatives, health, and educational factsheets.

4) www.pro-life.org

This site offers a variety of information regarding pro-life issues.

Endnotes

Chapter One

1. 410 U.S. 113 – Roe v. Wade

2. 410 U.S. 179 – Doe v. Bolton

3. 428 U.S. 52 – Danforth v. Missouri

4. L.D. Wardle & M.Q. Wood, *A Lawyer Looks at Abortion* (Provo, Utah: Brigham Young University Press, 1982).

5. J.P. Witherspoon, "Impact of the Abortion Decisions Upon the Father's Role," *The Jurist,* 35, 1975, p. 32-65.

6. A. Etzioni, "The Husband's Rights in Abortion," *Trial,* 12, 1976, p. 58.

7. B. Nathanson, *Aborting America* (New York: Doubleday, 1979) p. 257.

8. K. DeCrow, "Letter to the Editor," *New York Times Magazine,* May 9, 1982, p. 108.

9. A. Shostak & G. McLouth, *Men and Abortion: Lessons, Losses, and Love* (New York: Praeger, 1984).

10. R.A. Gordon & C. Kilpatrick, "A Program of Group Counseling for Men Who Accompany Women Seeking Legal Abortions," *Community Mental Health Journal,* 13 (4), 1977, p. 291-295.

11. Ibid., p. 293.

12. A. Shostak & G. McLouth, *Men and Abortion: Lessons, Losses, and Love* (New York: Praeger, 1984).

13. Ibid., p. 22.

14. J. Patterson, "Whose Freedom of Choice? Sometimes It Takes Two to Untangle," *The Progressive*, 46 (1), 1982, p. 42-45.

15. M. Buchanan & C. Robbins, "Early Adult Psychological Consequences for Males of Adolescent Pregnancy and Its Resolution," *Journal of Youth and Adolescence*, 19 (4), 1990, p. 413-424.

16. A. Shostak & G. McLouth, *Men and Abortion: Lessons, Losses, and Love* (New York: Praeger, 1984) p. 145.

17. Ibid., p. 153.

18. E. Milling, "The Men Who Wait," *Woman's Life*, April, 1975, p. 48-49, 69-71.

19. A. Shostak & G. McLouth, *Men and Abortion: Lessons, Losses, and Love* (New York: Praeger, 1984).

20. J. Mattinson, "The Effects of Abortion on a Marriage," Abortion: Medical Progress and Social Implications, *Ciba Foundation Symposium*, 115, 1985, p. 165-177.

21. V. Rue, *Forgotten Fathers: Men and Abortion* (Brochure published by Life Cycle Books, P.O. Box 420, Lewiston, NY 14092-0420) 1986.

22. Ibid.

23. Linda Bird, Francke, *The Ambivalence of Abortion* (New York: Random House, 1978).

24. J. Berger, "The Psychotherapeutic Treatment of Male Homosexuality," *American Journal of Psychotherapy*, 48 (2), 1994, p. 251.

25. A. Shostak & G. McLouth, *Men and Abortion: Lessons, Losses, and Love* (New York: Praeger, 1984).

26. Ibid.

Chapter Two

1. V.M. Rue, "The Effects of Abortion on Men," *Ethics and Medics*, 21 (4), 1996, p. 3-4.

2. V.M. Rue, "Postabortion Counselling," *British Journal of Sexual Medicine*, January/February, 1998, p. 26.

Chapter Three

1. C.T. Coyle & R.D. Enright, "Forgiveness Intervention With Post-abortion Men," *Journal of Consulting and Clinical Psychology*, 65 (6), 1997, p. 1042-1046.

2. L.B. Smedes, *Forgive and Forget: Healing the Hurts We Don't Deserve* (San Francisco: Harper & Row, 1984) p. 60.

3. J. North, J. "Wrongdoing and Forgiveness," *Philosophy*, 62, 1987, p. 499-508.

4. C.T. Coyle & R.D. Enright, "Forgiveness Education With Adult Learners," in *Adult Learning and Development: Perspectives From Educational Psychology*, M.C. Smith & T. Pourchot, eds. (Mahwah, NJ: Lawrence Erlbaum Associates, 1998) p. 219-238.

5. R.D. Enright & the Human Development Study Group, "Counseling Within the Forgiveness Triad: On Forgiving, Receiving Forgiveness, and Self-Forgiveness," *Counseling and Values*, 40, 1996, p. 107-146.

6. M.J. Subkoviak, R.D. Enright, C. Wu, E.A. Gassin, S. Freedman, L.M. Olson & I. Sarinopoulos, "Measuring Interpersonal Forgiveness in Late Adolescence and Middle Adulthood," *Journal of Adolescence*, 18, 1995, p. 641-655.

7. D.C. Reardon, *Aborted Women, Silent No More* (Chicago: Loyola University Press, 1987).

8. A.C. Speckhard & V.M. Rue, "Postabortion Syndrome: An Emerging Public Health Concern," *Journal of Social Issues*, 48 (3), 1992, p. 95-119.

9. Ibid.

10. A.E. Bergin, "Three Contributions of a Spiritual Perspective to Counseling, Psychotherapy, and Behavior Change," *Counseling and Values*, 33, 1988, p. 21-31.

11. R.D. Enright & the Human Development Study Group, "Counseling Within the Forgiveness Triad: On Forgiving, Receiving Forgiveness, and Self-forgiveness," *Counseling and Values,* 40, 1996, p. 107-146.

Chapter Four

All Scripture references are from the *NIV Study Bible, New International Version*, Grand Rapids: Zondervan.

1. Acts 10:43

2. Romans 3:22

3. Romans 3:23

4. Luke 11:4

5. Mark 11:25

6. Matthew 6:14-15

7. Ephesians 4:26

8. Matthew 18:15

9. 1 John 3:11

10. John 14:15

11. 2 John 6

12. John 3:16

13. Matthew 10:29-31

14. Luke 6:36

15. Ephesians 4:32

16. Ephesians 4:2

17. Psalm 68:19

18. Luke 7:47

19. Romans 8:28

20. Romans 3:23

21. 2 Corinthians 1:4

22. 2 Corinthians 2:7

Chapter Five

1. Ephesians 4:26, *NIV Study Bible, New International Version* (Grand Rapids: Zondervan).

2. R.P. Fitzgibbons, "The Cognitive and Emotive Use of Forgiveness in the Treatment of Anger," *Psychotherapy*, 23, 1986, p. 629-633.

3. Ibid., p. 630.

4. J.H. Hebl & R.D. Enright, "Forgiveness as a Psychotherapeutic Goal with Elderly Females," *Psychotherapy*, 30, 1993, p. 658-667.

5. R.H. Al-Mabuk, R.D. Enright & P.A. Cardis, "Forgiveness Education with Parentally Love-Deprived Late Adolescents," *Journal of Moral Education*, 24, 1995, p. 427-444.

6. S.R. Freedman & R.D. Enright, "Forgiveness as an Intervention Goal With Incest Survivors," *Journal of Consulting and Clinical Psychology*, 64, 1996, p. 983-992.

7. Romans 3:10, *NIV Study Bible, New International Version* (Grand Rapids: Zondervan).

Chapter Six

1. C.K. Benson, "Forgiveness and the Psychotherapeutic Process," *Journal of Psychology and Christianity*, 11 (1), 1992, p. 76-81.

Chapter Seven

1. W.H. Lewis, ed., *Letters of C.S. Lewis* (New York: Harcourt Brace Jovanovich, 1966) p. 230.

2. Luke 15:11-24, *NIV Study Bible, New International Version* (Grand Rapids: Zondervan).

Chapter Eight

1. A. Shostak & G. McLouth, *Men and Abortion: Lessons, Losses, and Love* (New York: Praeger, 1984).

2. E. Milling, "The Men Who Wait," *Woman's Life,* April, 1975, p. 48-49, 69-71.

Chapter Nine

1. V.M. Rue, "Postabortion Counselling," *British Journal of Sexual Medicine,* January/February, 1998.

2. A.C. Speckhard & V.M. Rue, "Post-abortion Syndrome: An Emerging Public Health Concern," *Journal of Social Issues,* 48 (3), 1992, p. 95.

3. R.C. Erikson, "Post-Abortion Syndrome as a Variant of Post-Traumatic Stress Disorder." Paper presented at the annual meeting of the Association of Interdisciplinary Research in Values and Social Change. Sacramento, CA, June 1990.

4. D.C. Reardon, *Aborted Women, Silent No More* (Chicago: Loyola University Press, 1987).

5. V.M. Rue, "The Forgotten Fathers: Men and Abortion," *Heartbeat*, Fall 1984, p. 19-21.

6. W.F. Brauning, "Men and Abortion: A Search for Understanding and Recovery," *Unpublished doctoral dissertation* (Westminster Theological Seminary, 1993).

7. V.M. Rue, "Postabortion Counselling," *British Journal of Sexual Medicine*, January/February, 1998.

8. V.M. Rue, "Post-abortion Syndrome: Sham or Emerging Crisis?" *National Right to Life News*, January 15, 1987.

9. A.C. Speckhard & V.M. Rue, "Post-abortion Syndrome:

An Emerging Public Health Concern," *Journal of Social Issues,* 48 (3), 1992, p. 95.

10. Mark 10:14,16, *NIV Study Bible, New International Version* (Grand Rapids: Zondervan).

11. H.J.M. Nouwen, *Here and Now: Living in the Spirit* (New York: Crossroad, 1994) p. 33.

Chapter Ten

1. V. Frankl, *Man's Search for Meaning: An Introduction to Logotherapy* (New York: Simon and Schuster, 1984) p. 117.

2. Ibid., p. 151.

3. 2 Corinthians 1:3-4, *The Living Bible* (Wheaton, Illinois: Tyndale House, 1978).

Appendix A

1. J.H. Hebl & R.D. Enright, "Forgiveness as a Psychotherapeutic Goal with Elderly Females," *Psychotherapy,* 30, 1993, p. 658-667.

2. R.H. Al-Mabuk, R.D. Enright & P.A. Cardis, "Forgiveness Education With Parentally Love-Deprived Late Adolescents," *Journal of Moral Education,* 24, 1995, p. 427-444.

3. S.R. Freedman & R.D. Enright, "Forgiveness as an Intervention Goal With Incest Survivors," *Journal of Consulting and Clinical Psychology,* 64, 1996, p. 983-992.

Appendix B

Bergin, A.E. "Three Contributions of a Spiritual Perspective to Counseling, Psychotherapy, and Behavioral Change." *Counseling and Values, 33*, 1988, p. 21-31.

Close, H.T. "Forgiveness and Responsibility: A Case Study." *Pastoral Psychology,* 21, 1970, p. 19-25.

Cunningham, B.B. "The Will to Forgive: A Pastoral Theological View of Forgiving." *The Journal of Pastoral Care,* 39, 1985, p. 141-149.

Droll, D.M. "Forgiveness: Theory and Research." *Unpublished doctoral dissertation.* University of Nevada-Reno, 1984.

Enright, R.D. & the Human Development Study Group. "The Moral Development of Forgiveness," in *Moral Behavior and Development,* W. Kurtines & J. Gewirtz, eds. (Vol. 1, p. 123-152). Hillsdale, NJ: Lawrence Erlbaum Associates, 1991.

Flanigan, B. *Forgiving.* Workshop presented at the Mendota Mental Health Institute, Madison, WI, September 25, 1987.

Frankl, V. *The Will to Meaning: Foundations and Applications of Logotherapy.* New York: World Publishing House, 1959.

Kiel, D.V. "I'm Learning How to Forgive." *Decisions,* February 1986, p. 12-13.

Neblett, W.R. "Forgiveness and Ideals." *Mind,* 83, 1974, p. 269-275.

North, J. "Wrongdoing and Forgiveness." *Philosophy,* 62, 1987, p. 499-508.

Patton, J. *Is Human Forgiveness Possible?* Nashville, TN: Abingdon, 1985.

Smedes, L.B. *Forgive and Forget: Healing the Hurts We Don't Deserve.* San Francisco, CA: Harper & Row, 1984.

Smith, M. "The Psychology of Forgiveness." *The Month,* 14, 1981, p. 301-307.

Trainer, M. "Forgiveness: Intrinsic, Role-expected, Expedient in the Context of Divorce." *Unpublished doctoral dissertation.* Boston University, 1981.